# BLUEPRINTS

## Christmas
## Art and Craft

**Jim Fitzsimmons**

**Rhona Whiteford**

**Stanley Thornes (Publishers) Ltd**

## Do you receive *BLUEPRINTS NEWS*?

Blueprints is an expanding series of practical teacher's ideas books and photocopiable resources for use in primary schools. Books are available for separate infant and junior age ranges for every core and foundation subject, as well as for an ever widening range of other primary teaching needs. These include **Blueprints Primary English** books and **Blueprints Resource Banks. Blueprints** are carefully structured around the demands of the National Curriculum in England and Wales, but are used successfully by schools and teachers in Scotland, Northern Ireland and elsewhere.

**Blueprints** provide:
- *Total curriculum coverage*
- *Hundreds of practical ideas*
- *Books specifically for the age range you teach*
- *Flexible resources for the whole school or for individual teachers*
- *Excellent photocopiable sheets – ideal for assessment and children's work profiles*
- *Supreme value.*

Books may be bought by credit card over the telephone and information obtained on **(01242) 577944**. Alternatively, photocopy and return this **FREEPOST** form to receive **Blueprints News**, our regular update on all new and existing titles. You may also like to add the name of a friend who would be interested in being on the mailing list.

First published in 1994 by
Stanley Thornes (Publishers) Ltd
© Text Jim Fitzsimmons and Rhona Whiteford 1994
© Illustrations ST(P) Ltd 1994

Illustrations by Rhona Whiteford

Applications for such permission should be addressed to the publishers:
Stanley Thornes (Publishers) Ltd
Ellenborough House
Wellington Street
CHELTENHAM GL50 1YD

Reprinted 1995

Typeset by Tech-Set, Gateshead, Tyne & Wear.
Printed in Great Britain at The Bath Press, Avon

A catalogue record for this book is available from the British Library.

ISBN 0–7487–1728–5

# CONTENTS

# CHECKLIST OF ACTIVITIES

## Cards
1 Opening cracker card
2 Party hat card
3 Four little snowmen
4 Robin on a log
5 Standing robin
6 Glittering candle
7 Printed glitter tree
8 Town by night
9 Cone star card
10 Golden tree
11 Holly wreath
12 A Victorian posy
13 Snow fan card
14 Rocking Santa card
15 Three kings pop-up card
16 Snowflake card
17 Present card
18 Christmas stocking pull-up card
19 Woven star
20 Santa's face hanging card
21 Christmas tree concertina card
22 Stained-glass window card
23 Nativity card

## Calendars
1 Christmas garland advent calendar
2 Egg box advent calendar
3 Star advent calendar
4 Clock calendar
5 Matchbox advent calendar
6 Christmas tree advent calendar
7 Hanging belt calendar
8 Quilling calendar
9 Paper cut-out calendar
10 Sequinned bird calendar
11 Bus calendar
12 Desk calendar
13 Clown calendar
14 House calendar
15 Paper sculpture calendar
16 Perpetual calendar
17 Collage calendar
18 Frottage calendar
19 Hot-air balloon calendar
20 Cylinder calendar
21 Antique metal plaque calendar
22 Santa's sack advent calendar

## Presents
1 Painted wooden spoon
2 Jar of chocolate cherries
3 Seasonal bookmark
4 A writing set
5 Pressed-flower gardening folder
6 Lavender bags
7 Seed brooch
8 Designer brooches
9 Stone paper weights
10 Designer mirror
11 Tiny Christmas stocking
12 Dinner candle lamp
13 Wooden key tidy
14 Trinket tub
15 Geometric picture frame
16 Barbecue candle
17 Marbled candlestick
18 Pot-pourri parcels
19 Mr Wobble toy
20 Glittering gift box
21 Piggy bank
22 Decorated paper bowl
23 Name plates

## Room and Tree Decorations
1 Ribbon rosettes
2 Window fan
3 Winter scene
4 Snow bird mobile
5 Father Christmas mobile
6 Christmas pinata
7 Kissing bunch
8 Large Christmas baubles
9 Starry chandeliers
10 Quilling stars
11 Snowflake wall hanging
12 Glittered pine cones
13 Cone stars
14 Rocking robin
15 Mini Christmas garland
16 Victorian garland
17 Glitter cork
18 Shiny spirals
19 Paper straw stars
20 Egg box bauble
21 Foil stars
22 Pasta bauble
23 Tree pom-pom
24 Sweet chain
25 Mr Snow

## Table Decorations
1 Father Christmas cone
2 Cone Christmas tree
3 Christmas castle table decoration
4 Plastic netting tree

iv

# INTRODUCTION

*Blueprints: Christmas Art and Craft* offers a wide range of ideas for art and craft activities based on a festive theme. It will enable teachers to provide the necessary resources so that their children can create any of the items described. The book is organised into various sections which contain ideas for cards, calendars, presents, table decorations, room and tree decorations, hats and masks, scenery and Christmas recipes.

All the activities in this book require a greater or lesser degree of adult supervision. They are intended to be used with children of primary school age. We have not given specific age groups, but within each section of the book there is a range of activities varying from very simple tasks to others requiring a greater degree of experience and skill in the handling of materials and equipment. We have left the selection of the activities to the individual teacher who can better determine which of the skills in a given task the children can attempt. Obviously some of the activities will require greater spans of concentration and involve several processes, and these will be more suitable for more experienced children. However, it is possible to organise the work so that even the youngest can tackle a long task if the job is broken up into several sessions. Examine carefully the skills involved in a task and help where necessary. Even apparently simple skills such as the handling of glue spreaders and paintbrushes can be improved with practice, making a vast difference to the finished product. Do try a variety of tasks so that the children gain experience of as many materials and techniques as possible.

Remember that observation and discussion form an integral part of these activities, and that much language development can result from even the simplest of tasks. During the cookery activities, encourage the children to observe and talk about the changes caused by mixing ingredients, and the effects of heating and cooling on different substances. Talking about the task in hand helps children to conceptualise their experiences.

Each activity includes a list of materials needed. These are the special items required for that particular task. Basic classroom equipment such as pens, pencils, scissors and sellotape are not listed but will need to be available for most tasks.

## Safety Aspects

When working with art and craft materials and equipment remember to be aware of the safety aspects governing their use. All dangerous substances and equipment should be stored well out of children's reach. These include such items as some adhesives, spray paint cans, craft knives, pointed scissors, and very small craft materials (for example, seeds, pulses, buttons and sequins) which could become lodged in ears, noses or eyes. Remind the children not to put any objects in their mouth, and not to poke friends with sharp craft materials. Even art straws can cause damage if poked in an eye. Do be aware of the possibility of allergic reaction to certain foods if you prepare any of the recipes.

Remember that spray paints and strong adhesives should be used outside or in a well-ventilated area. Always clean up spillages immediately: adhesives, paint and sand can cause someone to slip.

Encourage safety awareness in the children by, for example, getting them to spot potential dangers in materials or equipment left unattended. Teach them to carry equipment such as scissors in a safe manner. Children of all ages readily absorb safety advice in their code of rules and can be helpful in maintaining safety standards if they understand their importance.

# CARDS

## ACTIVITY 1: OPENING CRACKER CARD

**Materials needed**

Strips of card (40 cm × 12 cm) in dark red, dark blue or white; potatoes; ready-mixed powder paint; assorted bits of coloured foil; glue.

**What to do**

Prepare the potato printing blocks by cutting some very simple shapes. Older children can do this for themselves by cutting the potato in half then using the cut surface from which to make the printing shape. Pour a little paint into a shallow container. The printing block is dipped in this so that it is covered sparingly. Alternatively, a thin sheet of sponge can be added to the container to absorb excess paint when the block is pressed on it.

Fold the strips of card as shown and cut the ends into cracker shapes. Taking care not to get paint on the front, print an all-over design or pattern of the artist's choice on the inside. When this is dry, fold to close and add two strips of coloured foil and any other decoration to the ends of the cracker. Write a greeting on a piece of coloured paper (perhaps using a metallic felt-tip pen) and stick this centrally inside the card.

Cut out a simple shape … or cut block to shape.

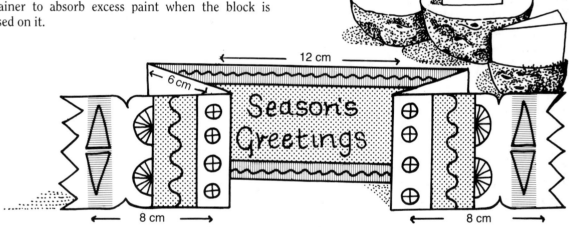

## ACTIVITY 2: PARTY HAT CARD

**Materials needed**

Coloured card (26 cm × 15 cm); cotton wool pom-poms; glue; assorted coloured foil.

**What to do**

Fold the card in half. Using the folded edge as one side, draw and cut out an equilateral triangle. Stand the triangle up on one of its open edges as the hat shape. Next cut out five or six strips of assorted coloured foil, approximately 8 cm × 1 cm, and staple them together at one end. Using a little glue, fix three small cotton wool pom-poms to the front of the card and then the stapled end of the streamers to the inside of the top point. Tidy up the inside of the card by sticking a small circle of coloured card over the ends of the streamers. Add a greeting to complete the card.

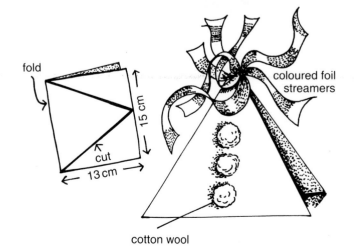

1

# ACTIVITY 3: FOUR LITTLE SNOWMEN

**Materials needed**

White card (40 cm × 15 cm); assorted scraps of coloured paper and foil; glue.

**What to do**

Fold the card into a concertina of four equal parts. Keeping it folded, draw a snowman shape on the top sheet and cut it out through the four sheets. Take care not to cut through the fold since this will be a hinge. An adult will need to do the cutting out for younger children.

Now the children can cut the scraps of coloured paper and foil to decorate each of the snowmen in a different way. Let them tear paper to create a ragged effect. They may need help with cutting long narrow strips, particularly when using vinyl foil papers. The decorations can be glued on as they are selected. A greeting can be written on the reverse side.

# ACTIVITY 4: ROBIN ON A LOG

**Materials needed**

Brown art paper; brown and red wool; black art paper; silver sequins; thick card; brown card; glue.

**What to do**

First of all make the pom-pom discs by cutting two circles (10 cm diameter) from the thick card, with a 3 cm hole in the centre of each one. Using the red wool first, wind it round about a third of the discs then complete the circle with brown wool, winding as thickly and as tightly as possible. Cut the wool, remove the discs and tie the pom-pom as shown.

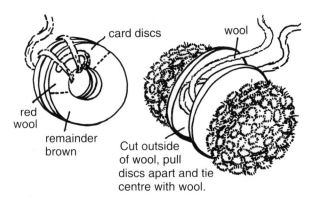

*Making the pom-pom*

2

Next cut out the beak, feet and tail from the brown card and fix these to the pom-pom body with a little glue. The eyes are made by gluing a small circle of black paper to the centre of each silver sequin. These are then fixed to the head with glue to complete the bird.

Make the log base from a piece of brown card, 15 cm × 10 cm, folded lengthways. The greeting can be written in silver metallic pen. Put a little glue on the centre of the fold and sit the robin on this.

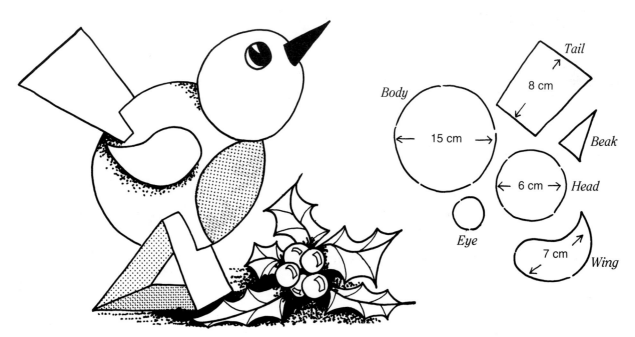

*Tail*

↑
3 cm
↓

*Feet × 2*

↑
2 cm
↓

*Beak*

black card

large silver sequin

*Eye*

5 cm

Happy Christmas

15 cm

---

# ACTIVITY 5: STANDING ROBIN

**Materials needed**
Brown and black card; red paint; thick card; glue.

**What to do**
An adult or older child should first make a set of templates as shown. The card makers can draw round them on brown card (using black card for eye and beak) and then cut out the pieces. Younger children may need help with the cutting.

Next paint a semi-circle of red on the larger circle to represent the red breast. When this is dry the robin can be assembled, using a little glue. To fix the tail, put a dot of glue on the robin's back, cut a slit in the base of the tail and slot it on to the glue. A message can be written on a small piece of paper and the paper glued to the reverse of the bird. Finally, fold a piece of card to make a stand, 21 cm × 3 cm, cut a slit in the top and slot the body on to it.

*Body*

15 cm

*Eye*

*Tail*

8 cm

*Beak*

← 6 cm → *Head*

7 cm

*Wing*

# ACTIVITY 6: GLITTERING CANDLE

**Materials needed**

Red card; red glitter; PVA glue; gold and silver foil paper.

**What to do**

Fold the card in half lengthways and cut a flame shape at one end. It should now be opened out to be worked on. Take a glue spreader full of glue and allow it to trail in thin lines in all directions over the whole of the opened out card except for the flame shapes. The glue can be dribbled in horizontal or vertical lines to make a pattern if desired. Now sprinkle red glitter liberally over the card and tap off the excess on to a sheet of clean paper.

To complete the card, cut out two large flame shapes in gold foil paper and two smaller shapes in silver, and glue on to each flame shape on the card.

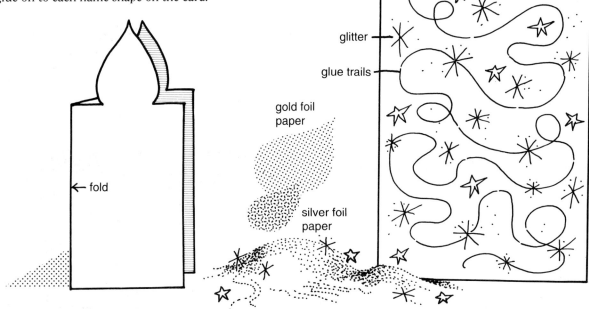

red card

glitter

glue trails

gold foil paper

silver foil paper

fold

# ACTIVITY 7: PRINTED GLITTER TREE

**Materials needed**

Dark green art paper; two shades of light green paint; triangles of sponge of the same size for printing blocks; star-shape and rectangular sponges; red, gold and green glitter; Copydex adhesive.

**What to do**

Make a stand-up card from the green paper in whatever size is preferred. Cut a curved top edge as shown. The shape of a Christmas tree can now be printed using the triangular sponges. Vary the shade of green paint used. When the paint is thoroughly dry, print over three or four triangles with the glue and then liberally sprinkle green glitter over them. Glue print the star and the plant pot with the star-shape and rectangular sponges and add red glitter for the pot and gold for the star. Sprinkle the glitter for each separately and tip off the excess each time so that the colours don't mix.

# ACTIVITY 8: TOWN BY NIGHT

**Materials needed**
Black card (36 cm × 15 cm); yellow, orange and red paper; silver glitter; glue.

**What to do**
First of all fold the card lengthways into three equal pieces, then cut the rooftops to make a diagonal slope as shown. Fold the card so that the tallest houses are at the back.

To add snow to the rooftops, first put a piece of scrap paper between the folds to keep the glue only where it is needed. A thin line of glue can then be drawn along the roof tops and sprinkled liberally with glitter. Shake off excess on to clean paper. The message can be written on lighter coloured paper and stuck in the lower part of the tallest group of houses, to be seen when the card is opened in the conventional way.

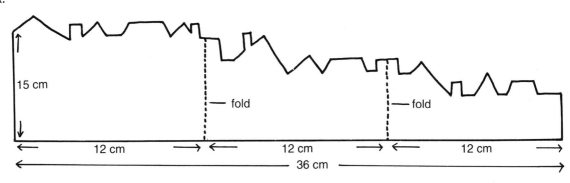

Now cut a variety of rectangles for windows from the orange and yellow paper and two or three rectangles for doors from the red paper. Keeping the card folded, stick a few windows on the houses at the back and the centre, and put doors and windows on the houses at the front.

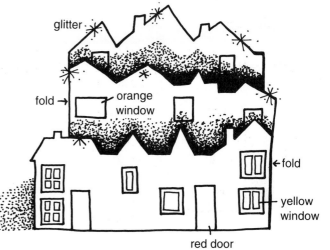

# ACTIVITY 9: CONE STAR CARD

**Materials needed**
Red card; white card; red and green double-sided foil; glue.

**What to do**
Take a piece of red card, 30 cm × 15 cm, and fold it in half to make a square. Stick a circle of white card, 15 cm in diameter, on the front.

To make the cones, cut out twelve 5 cm squares in the double-sided foil, six in one colour and six in the other. Hold one corner and fold the two points on either side towards each other to form a cone. Secure them with a little glue. To set the cones on the circle, draw a cross on the circle and use this as a guide to set three cones in each quadrant.

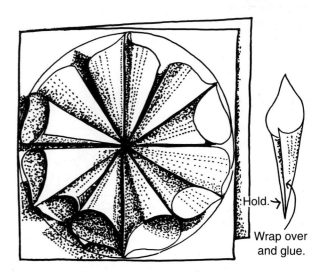

Hold.→

Wrap over and glue.

# ACTIVITY 10: GOLDEN TREE

**Materials needed**

White card; art straws; assorted coloured sequins; glue; gold spray paint.

**What to do**

Make a stand-up card about 15 cm × 20 cm. Cut one art straw about 18 cm long, brush a little glue along it and stick it on to the card as the vertical stem of the tree. Cut assorted lengths of art straws and stick these horizontally as branches.

When the glue is dry, spray the whole of the front of the card with gold spray paint (remember to do this in a well-ventilated area). When this is dry, decorate the branches with sequins, reserving a star for the top. Sequins are difficult to hold and the best method is to dot the glue on the branch then pop the sequin on to it.

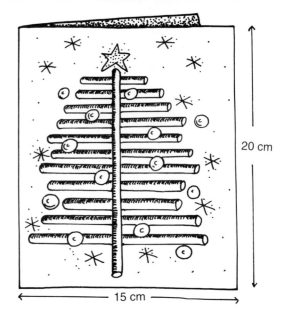

20 cm

←——— 15 cm ———→

# ACTIVITY 11: HOLLY WREATH

**Materials needed**

Green or brown card; green foil paper and green art paper; red foil paper; small piece of white card; silver glitter; metallic felt-tip pen; red parcel ribbon; glue.

**What to do**

Cut out a circle of card, either 20 cm or 30 cm depending on how big you want the finished card to be. Now cut holly leaves about 5–6 cm long, in both the art paper and the foil paper. You can cut several at once by folding your paper into the size needed and cutting through all the layers. You may need about thirty leaves in all, depending on the size of the ring and how closely together you put the leaves.

To prepare the leaves, fold them along their length and then open out to give a 3D effect. Brush a little glue along the bottom half of the back (convex edge) and fix it to the wreath circle. Fix two rows of leaves around the wreath, with the inner edges of the leaves glued down. If you also position some leaves overlapping the rows and add some circles of red for holly berries, a most realistic effect will be achieved.

To complete the card add a loop of red ribbon to the top, sellotaped at the back. A greeting can be written in metallic felt-tip pen on a small piece of card and the edge of the card rimmed in glitter (dip it in glue and then glitter) then sellotaped to the wreath.

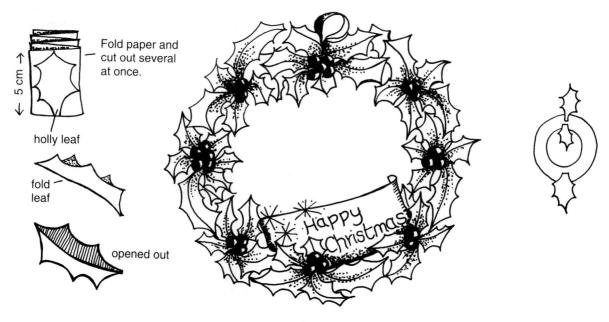

5 cm

Fold paper and cut out several at once.

holly leaf

fold leaf

opened out

# ACTIVITY 12: A VICTORIAN POSY

**Materials needed**

Dark green card; a collection of old Christmas cards; glue; narrow red ribbon; paper cake decoration bearing the words 'Season's Greetings'.

**What to do**

Make a square card and then cut the top edge into curves to give a fluted effect. For the montage, search through old Christmas cards for small motifs of flowers or seasonal shrubs and leaves and small decorations like candles and baubles. Cut them out carefully.

Using a circular template, draw a circle on the front of the card with a pencil and take this as a guide for positioning the motifs to make a pleasing arrangement. Stick the motifs in place with a little glue and add the cake decoration greeting in the centre. To complete the card, make a small bow of red ribbon and glue it at the bottom of the posy.

# ACTIVITY 13: SNOW FAN CARD

**Materials needed**

White card; silver foil paper; white paper; Copydex adhesive.

**What to do**

Cut a circle of card 15 cm in diameter and fold it in half with a good crease so that it will rock on its curved edge. Next cut a piece of foil paper 40 cm × 7 cm and pleat it as for a paper fan into folds approximately 1 cm wide. Staple this at the top to secure the fan and open it out to the shape of the semi-circular card. Position the open fan on the card and fix it with a staple at either side, inside a fold, as shown. Fix the centre of the fan to the card with a little contact adhesive such as Copydex.

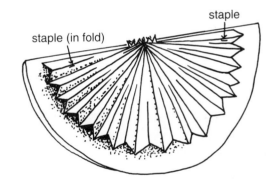

You will now need about five small white paper snowflakes. To make them, cut circles of white paper 3 cm in diameter, fold into six and cut a small shape through the layers. You will need a sharp pair of scissors to cut such a tiny shape. Position the snowflakes on the fan and secure with a tiny spot of Copydex to the ridges of the paper. Put one snowflake at the top to cover the stapled centre of the fan.

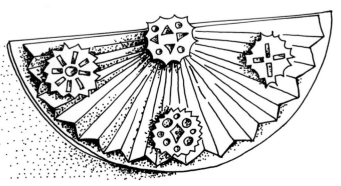

7

# ACTIVITY 14: ROCKING SANTA CARD

**Materials needed**
White card; silver glitter; glue.

**What to do**
Cut a circle of card 15 cm in diameter and fold it in half with a good crease. Stand it on its edge to make a rocking card. Now take a piece of card 15 cm square and, using the curved edge of the rocking card as a template, draw the same curve on the bottom half of this and cut it out. This curve will be the rocker on Santa's chair. Draw a faint pencil line down the centre of the card as a guide so that the figure can be drawn as equally as

possible on each side to balance the card. If the figure is too much to one side the card will constantly rock over and rest on that side. Draw the figure in pencil and then colour it in with felt pens. Cut out the figure and leave the curved edge intact. Add glitter to the fur on Santa's clothes by brushing those areas with glue and then sprinkling glitter on this.

The figure on its chair can now be glued to the rocker. The glue should be put on the card rocker; if you use a slow-drying glue like PVA there will be enough mobility to allow you to adjust the position of the rocker curve to the card curve so that a good balance is achieved.

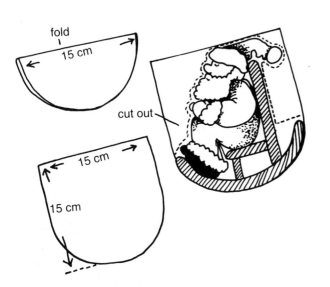

# ACTIVITY 15: THREE KINGS POP-UP CARD

**Materials needed**
Yellow card (20 cm × 24 cm); blue art paper (20 cm × 14 cm); white card; silver foil paper; glue.

**What to do**
Fold the yellow card in half to make a folded card 20 cm × 12 cm. Working on the folded edge, cut six slits, as shown. Open out the card and pull the three cut tabs to the inside of the card so that they form upright brackets when the card is standing on its side. Cut a strip off the top of the vertical edge in a curved shape to represent sand dunes in the desert.

To make the kings, cut three pieces of white card 5 cm × 7 cm and draw a figure on each with felt pens, leaving the bottom edge straight. Cut out the figures. Put a little glue on the vertical face of the brackets and fix a king to each. The desert sky can now be added by lightly gluing the blue art paper to the back of the card. Cut a star out of foil paper and fix it to the sky to complete the picture. A greeting can be written on the desert sand at the kings' feet.

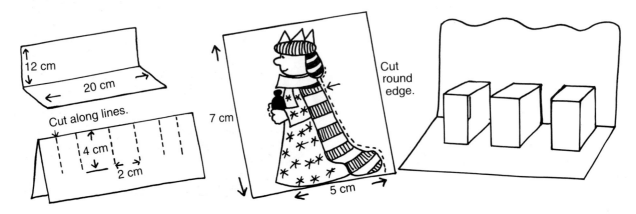

Happy Christmas to Mum and Dad love Sue

# ACTIVITY 16: SNOWFLAKE CARD

**Materials needed**

Dark blue card; silver and red foil paper; glue.

**What to do**

Cut a piece of card 18 cm × 36 cm and fold into a square. Now draw a 13 cm diameter circle on the centre of one of the squares and cut it out carefully. To do this neatly, pierce the centre of the card with scissors and then cut towards the curved edge and into it. Next cut a 15 cm diameter circle from the silver foil paper. Fold it in half and then in thirds in order to cut out a six-sided snowflake. Stick this over the hole in the front of the card but use only a tiny bit of glue on each of the extremities.

To complete the card, cut a 15 cm diameter circle from the red foil paper and stick this on the inside of the card so that the colour shows through the holes in the snowflake.

# ACTIVITY 17: PRESENT CARD

**Materials needed**

Small cuboid box; Christmas wrapping paper; coloured card; white card; parcel ribbon; glue.

**What to do**

Wrap up the small box to look like a Christmas present and tie the ribbon round it with a neat bow on the front. Make a small label from a piece of coloured card and write on it the name of the person to whom the card will be sent. Now cut a rectangular card the same size as the 'present' and write a greeting inside, as for a conventional card. Spread glue over the whole of the back of the box and stick it on to the card.

# ACTIVITY 18: CHRISTMAS STOCKING PULL-UP CARD

**Materials needed**
White card (20 cm × 30 cm); white paper; cotton wool; glue; scraps of foil paper.

**What to do**
Fold the card in half to make an upright card 20 cm × 15 cm. Draw the shape of a Christmas stocking on the front, but leave about 5 cm space at the top for the 'pull' and the cotton wool 'fur'. Cut a slit across the top of the stocking. Draw patterns on the stocking with brightly coloured pens and glue on bits of foil paper if desired.

Glue cotton wool across the top to hide the slit. Write a seasonal greeting with metallic felt pen.

To make the pull-up mechanism cut a piece of card as wide as the top of the stocking and as long as the heel to top measurement plus a 2 cm 'pull' handle. Make the bottom of the card a little wider to prevent it being pulled out altogether. A collection of presents can be drawn on the card. Cut around the top edge of the presents and slot the card into position. To secure it on the reverse of the Christmas card, stick on a piece of paper to make a pocket. Complete the card with a message on the inside.

# ACTIVITY 19: WOVEN STAR

**Materials needed**
Gold and silver foil paper; white card; red card; glue.

**What to do**
Cut five strips of silver foil and five strips of gold foil, all 1 cm × 16 cm. Weave them together as shown and add dabs of glue to the backs of the strips to keep them in place. Trim each end of the star into a 'V' and stick the whole star on to an 18 cm square of red card. Trim the card to outline the star shape. Cut out an 18 cm square of white card and attach the red card to it, using sellotape hinges. The message can be written on the white card.

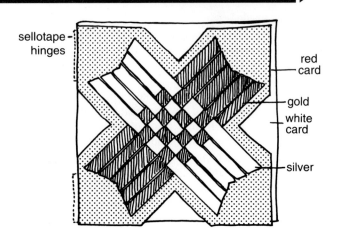

10

# ACTIVITY 20: SANTA'S FACE HANGING CARD

**Materials needed**
Small white paper plate; red and white paper; cotton wool; PVA glue; silver glitter; red parcel ribbon.

**What to do**
Turn the plate over and work on the back. Cut out a nose from the red paper. Cut out two circles for eyes from the white paper and use felt-tip pens to draw eyes, leaving a rim of white round the edge as shown. These features will be stuck on the face after the hat, hair and beard are in place.

Cut out a triangle from the red paper for Santa's hat and stick this at the top of the paper plate. To make the beard, take a piece of white paper about 40 cm long and as wide as the paper plate. Use the edge of the plate as a template to draw a curve on each end, as shown, and then cut out these curves carefully. Fold the paper into pleats about 1 cm wide, then fix it to the bottom of the paper plate with a little glue. Cotton wool 'fur' can now be added to the hat and some more placed at the top of the beard and round the edge of the face. Brush the glue on the plate sparingly and tease out the cotton wool before sticking it down in fairly loose, long pieces to give the fluffiest effect. Trail the cotton wool down the beard a little.

Now stick the features on to the face and add eyebrows and mouth with a black felt-tip pen. Add a little cotton wool on top of the mouth for the moustache. For the finishing touch dribble fine lines of PVA glue in twirling movements all over the beard. Sprinkle glitter on to the glue and shake off excess downwards to avoid the cotton wool.

*To make the beard:*

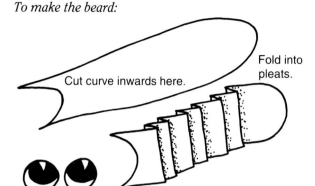

Cut curve inwards here.

Fold into pleats.

Draw eyes with felt-tipped pen.

To complete the card, sellotape a loop of red parcel ribbon to the back of the hat at the top so that the card can be hung up. Write a greeting on the inside of the paper plate.

cotton wool

glue and glitter

# ACTIVITY 21: CHRISTMAS TREE CONCERTINA CARD

**Materials needed**
Dark green card (36 cm × 15 cm); green foil paper; assorted coloured sequins; yellow art paper (20 cm × 5 cm); glue; scraps of brown and red foil paper.

**What to do**
Fold the card lengthways into three equal pieces, as shown. Draw a fir tree shape on the back of the green foil and cut it out; it should be about 12 cm tall and about 12 cm at its widest point. Glue this to the centre front of the card and add a trunk and a pot from scraps of foil paper. Leave the glue to dry thoroughly then use a ruler to draw a vertical line at the centre of the top and bottom of the card. Carefully cut out half the tree shape, following the dotted line shown. The tree can now be decorated with sequins stuck on with glue. The easiest

way is to dot the glue on to the tree first and then add the tiny decorations to it.

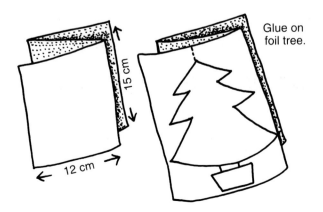

15 cm

12 cm

Glue on foil tree.

11

The concertina greeting is made by taking the yellow art paper and folding it into 1 cm pleats. Open it out again and cut zig-zags as wide as the pleats along the bottom edge. The greeting can be written on the pleats, using one space for each letter, but leaving the first and last pleats for fixing the concertina to the card. You can add any other decorations in felt-tip pen at this stage. Refold the concertina and fix it inside the card by means of a little glue on the end pleats.

Cut out left-hand edge of tree on first fold.

# ACTIVITY 22: STAINED-GLASS WINDOW CARD

**Materials needed**
Grey and black art paper; assorted coloured foil paper; glue; paper cake decoration.

**What to do**
Cut out a church window shape in the black art paper, about 12 cm × 15 cm, and then make a rectangular card from the grey art paper so that the folded card is about 17 cm square. Draw some simple patterns on the black window shape, using a ruler for the straight lines. You will need to leave a border around the edge of at least 2 cm. Cut these shapes out carefully. Now use scraps of coloured foil to fill the cut-out shapes, allowing a little overlap so that they can be glued on the inside of the card. It is best to brush glue around one hole at a time and add the foil infill before going on to the next. Plan the colours carefully so that they complement each other.

Now spread glue lightly round the edge of the window's back and stick it on to the grey card, leaving a deeper space at the bottom. To add some colour and a 3D effect you can put ivy leaves over the edge of the windowsill. Cut a piece of green foil about 25 cm × 4 cm and fold it into five or six equal pieces. Draw an ivy leaf on it and cut through all the layers. Fold each leaf along the three spines and partly open out again. The leaves can be stuck on with a dot of glue at the bottom and at the tip of each leaf. Overlap the leaves, starting from the top so that they look as though they are growing from the bottom upwards. A paper cake decoration greeting can be added to give a professional touch.

cut-out shapes for glass

2 cm rim

Fold leaves along these lines.

15 cm

12 cm

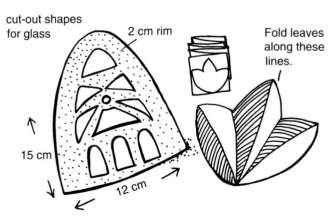

12

# ACTIVITY 23: NATIVITY CARD

**Materials needed**

Thin wool in yellow and beige; black card (22 cm × 15 cm); white paper; silver foil paper; glue.

**What to do**

Take the black card and cut and fold it as shown. Now cut a piece of white paper to fit the rectangle which will form the back of the stable and use felt pens to draw a picture of the holy family with the crib in the stable.

Cut the wool into strips long enough to cover the stable roof. Spread glue across the roof then lay the wool in mixed colour stripes. Trim the top and bottom edges. Make a plait of six strips of wool long enough to stretch across the width of the roof and stick this about 1 cm below the apex. Cut out a foil star and glue it to the thatched roof. Next cut a small window in one of the side walls and write a greeting on the other side. To finish the card, stick the picture on the back wall, open out the walls and lower the roof on to them. Display the card on a table with vases of evergreens.

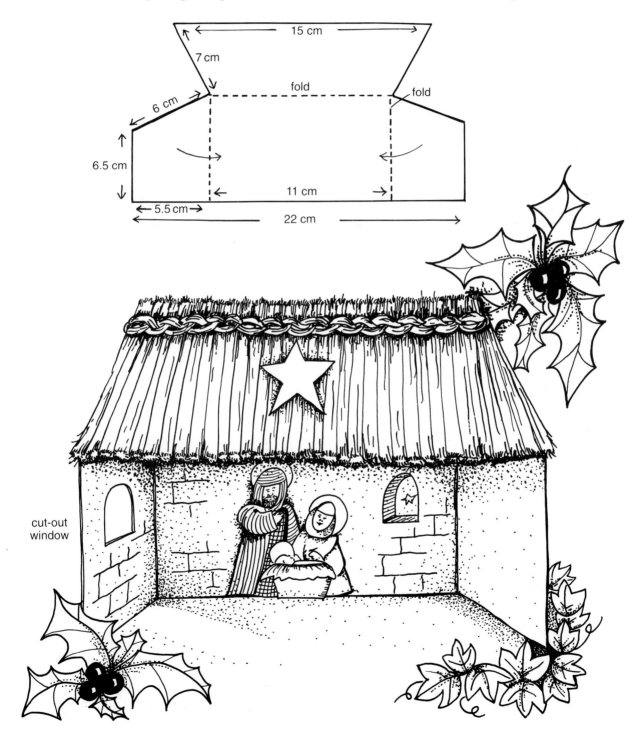

# CALENDARS

## ACTIVITY 1: CHRISTMAS GARLAND ADVENT CALENDAR

**Materials needed**

Small PE hoop; green crêpe paper; green paper for holly leaves; red or tartan ribbon; sweets; foil paper in red, green or gold; glue.

**What to do**

Cut the green crêpe paper into strips and wrap them around the hoop, fastening the ends with a little glue. Cut out large holly leaf shapes and glue these to the covered hoop to look like a Christmas wreath. Cut twenty-four squares of foil paper (about 10 cm square). Put a few sweets on each and twist to make a parcel. Wrap a long piece of wool around the top and fasten it tight. Leave two long ends of wool to fasten the parcel to the garland. Number the parcels 1 to 24 and tie them to the hoop.

Hang the Advent garland in a place where the children can reach it safely. On the first day of December a child can untie the parcel with the number 1 on it, and on each subsequent day the parcel with the number that corresponds to the date may be taken down and opened, thus marking the passing of Advent.

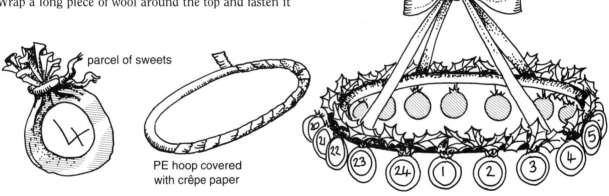

parcel of sweets

PE hoop covered with crêpe paper

## ACTIVITY 2: EGG BOX ADVENT CALENDAR

**Materials needed**

Tissue paper; four egg boxes; circular adhesive labels; paint; small pictures cut from old Christmas cards; tinsel or crêpe paper; glue.

**What to do**

Sellotape the four egg boxes together, as shown. Paint them a bright colour. Cut small circular pictures from old Christmas cards, large enough to cover the bottom of each section of the egg cartons.

Glue the pictures in place. Drop a sweet into each section and then cover the whole surface of the cartons with a sheet of tissue paper. Now number the adhesive labels 1 to 24 and fix one over each section. Decorate the whole thing with a crêpe frill or scraps of tinsel. Stand or hang the box in a suitable place so that the children can pierce the tissue around the appropriate number to mark the passing of the days of Advent.

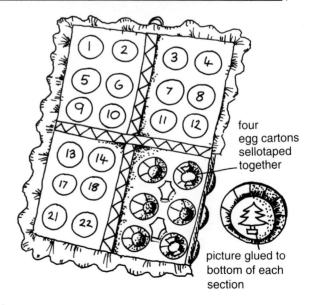

four egg cartons sellotaped together

picture glued to bottom of each section

14

# ACTIVITY 3: STAR ADVENT CALENDAR

**Materials needed**

White card; old Christmas cards; plasticene; twenty-four thin garden canes or plant stakes; glue; ribbon or tinsel; cake board or paper plate; holly or other evergreens.

**What to do**

Take a large lump of plasticene and place it on a flat cake board or paper plate. Cut out twenty-four pictures from old Christmas cards, each approximately 4 cm across, and cut out twenty-four circles of the same size from the white card. Mark each white circle with a number from 1 to 24, using a marker pen. Glue a picture and a white circle to one end of each cane, with the picture and the number both facing outwards.

Stick the other ends of the canes into the plasticene in a circle, as shown, with the numbers on top. To disguise the plasticene in the middle push in sprigs of holly or other available evergreens and decorate with ribbon or tinsel. To mark the passing of Advent, a child finds the number that corresponds to the date and turns the cane over to reveal the Christmas picture.

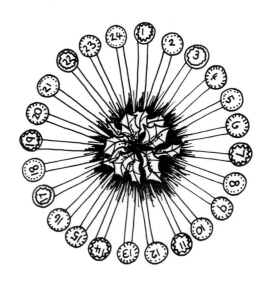

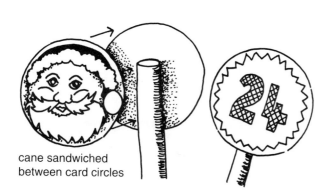

cane sandwiched
between card circles

# ACTIVITY 4: CLOCK CALENDAR

**Materials needed**

Large white paper plate; red, yellow and blue card; paper fastener; piece of string about 10 cm long.

**What to do**

Draw four circles on the plate using compasses, or circular templates of different sizes. Leave the middle of the plate and the outer rim blank. Use different coloured felt-tip pens when writing in each circle. Starting from the outside, in the first circle write the names of the months. Fit three months in each quarter of the plate, starting with January at the top. In the next circle write the names of the days of the week; try to space them out evenly, starting with Monday at the top. In the third circle write the dates, from 1 to 31.

Make the clock hands by cutting a strip of red card long enough to reach from the middle of the plate to the months, then a strip of yellow card, long enough to reach the days, and finally a strip of blue card for the dates. Cut a point at one end of each strip. At the opposite end make a hole and push the strips on to a paper fastener, starting with blue, then yellow, then red. Push the fastener through the centre of the plate and open it at the back. You could decorate the rim of the calendar by drawing a pattern, or sticking on sequins, seeds or pasta.

Make a loop of string and fix it to the back of the clock with sellotape, then hang the calendar on the wall. Every day move the blue hand to show the date and the yellow hand to show the day. You will need to move the red hand only on the first day of each new month.

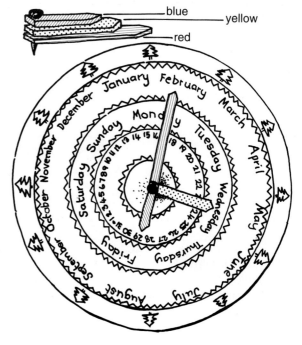

15

# ACTIVITY 5: MATCHBOX ADVENT CALENDAR

## Materials needed

Card (46 cm × 40 cm); gold foil paper (same size); twenty-four empty matchboxes; glitter; tinsel and paper ribbon; glue; twenty-four sweets or small gifts; coloured foil; old Christmas card; glitter pens.

## What to do

Cover the rectangle of card with the gold foil paper. Next cut the coloured foil into strips the same width as the matchboxes and long enough to wrap around them. Coat the back of the strips with glue and wrap around each matchbox. Use a little tinsel to decorate the ends of the matchboxes then position them on the gold card in six rows of four and glue them in place. Place a sheet of cardboard over the top of the matchboxes and weight it down with a few books. Leave them to dry. Using the glitter pens, number the matchboxes from 1 to 24 and put a sweet or a small gift inside each one.

Decorate the calendar by cutting a picture from an old Christmas card and gluing it along the top. Fix some ribbon or tinsel around the edge of the calendar with glue and make a loop at the back to hang it up.

# ACTIVITY 6: CHRISTMAS TREE ADVENT CALENDAR

## Materials needed

Large sheet of paper (or several sheets joined together), as large as you want the tree to be, but at least 1.5 m by 1 m for best effect; sponges; green paint; scraps of tinsel and coloured foil; twenty-four envelopes; old Christmas cards; thin stiff card.

## What to do

Draw the outline of a Christmas tree, with trunk and pot, on the sheet of paper. Let the children sponge paint the surface until the outline is completely covered, then leave to dry. When it is dry cut out the tree.

Cut twenty-four rectangles from the stiff card, large enough to fit lengthways inside the envelopes. Cut out pictures from the old Christmas cards and glue one to the top half of each piece of card, with the shortest edge of the card at the top. Close the flap of each envelope and decorate the back, incorporating in the design on the flap a number from 1 to 24. Glue the envelopes on to the tree and decorate the spaces between the envelopes with scraps of tinsel and coloured foil. Place a gold star at the top. The tree can now be pinned or stapled to a wall or a display board.

The flaps of the envelopes are opened on the appropriate dates and the cards inside placed upright so that the Christmas picture shows. The stiff card will hold the flap of the envelope up.

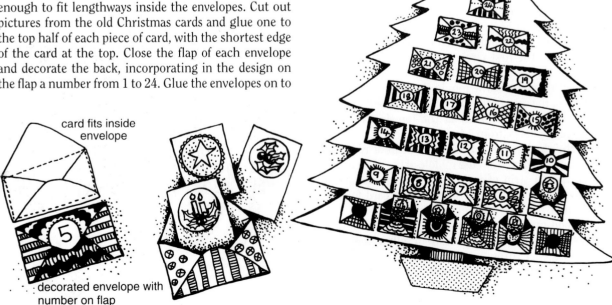

card fits inside
envelope

decorated envelope with
number on flap

16

# ACTIVITY 7: HANGING BELT CALENDAR

## Materials needed

Strip of card 72 cm × 8 cm; rectangle of card 6 cm × 12 cm; large paper clip; velcro strip; thick marker pen; glue; white card; string or wool.

## What to do

Glue the rectangle of card to one end of the card strip. Decorate the rectangle to look like the buckle of a belt. Mark off the strip below the buckle into thirty-one equal sections of 2 cm each and number them 1 to 31. Cut out twelve rectangles of card to fit inside the buckle design (about 6 cm × 4 cm). On each card write the name of a month.

Stick a 3 cm strip of the felt side of the velcro on to the back of each month card, then stick a 3 cm strip of the hooked side on to the centre of the buckle design.

The month is displayed by fixing the appropriate card inside the buckle. The date is shown by sliding the large paper clip over the appropriate number on the belt. To finish off the calendar, cut the end of the belt into a pointed shape and draw two holes. Fix a loop of string or wool to the back of the buckle so that the belt can be hung.

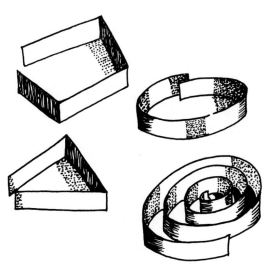

# ACTIVITY 8: QUILLING CALENDAR

## Materials needed

Circle of card, cut to required size but with radius at least 3 cm larger than the calendar pad; coloured activity paper; calendar pad; glue; ribbon.

## What to do

Place the calendar pad in the centre of the card circle and draw around it, then remove it. Cut the activity paper into strips 2 cm wide and fold or curve to make squares, circles, spirals or triangles. To make a spiral, wind a strip of paper around a pencil, a paintbrush or any other long, thin, cylindrical shape. Remove the curled paper gently and tease it into shape.

These shapes can be glued around the edge of the card circle to create a 3D effect. Make sure that the outline shape of the calendar pad is left clear. When all the shapes are fixed in place, glue the calendar pad in the outline. Loop a length of ribbon on the back of the calendar and hang it up.

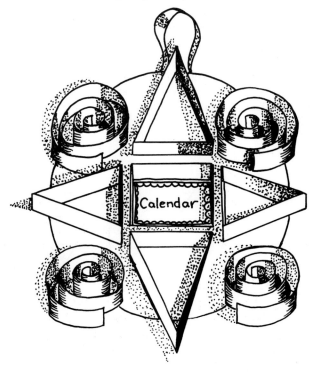

17

# ACTIVITY 9: PAPER CUT-OUT CALENDAR

### Materials needed
Coloured activity paper (20 cm × 12 cm); glue; card (28 cm × 18 cm); calendar pad; ribbon or cord.

### What to do
Fold the rectangle of coloured paper lengthways down the centre. Make pairs of diagonal cuts along the folded edge. Open up the rectangle once again and fold the cuts chevron shape out and downwards.

Glue the cut-out paper on to the rectangle of card, leaving space at the bottom to glue on the calendar pad. Attach a loop of ribbon or cord at the top of the calendar, at the back, to enable it to be hung.

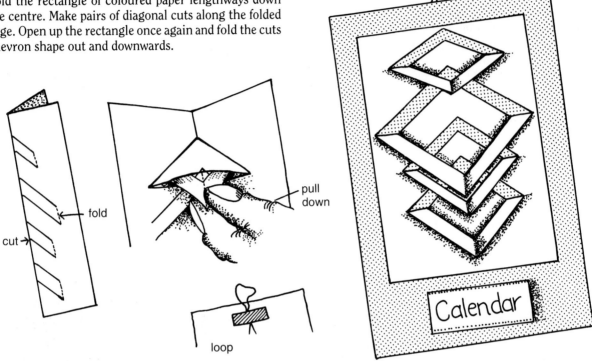

# ACTIVITY 10: SEQUINNED BIRD CALENDAR

### Materials needed
Thin stiff card; brightly coloured or silver sequins; calendar pad; glue; small magnet; bird-shaped template for younger children.

### What to do
Draw and cut out a simple bird shape. Younger children can use a template to draw around. This activity provides useful practice in fine motor control and hand–eye co-ordination. If possible, let the children cut out their own shape. You will need to bear this in mind when choosing the card: if it is too stiff they will have difficulty in cutting. Once the shape has been drawn and cut out, glue the calendar pad into place in the centre and decorate the outer edge of the bird with sequins. Glue a small magnet on to the back so that the calendar can be placed on the door of a fridge.

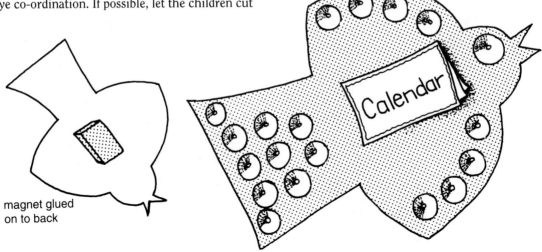

magnet glued on to back

# ACTIVITY 11: BUS CALENDAR

**Materials needed**

Small rectangular cardboard box; white paper; calendar pad; photographs of the child and family, if possible; PVA glue; paint; empty matchbox; strong card discs, plastic bottle tops or coffee jar lids.

**What to do**

Seal the box ends and glue white paper over the open end. Paint the box all over with a mixture of two parts paint to one part adhesive. This helps the paint to stick to waxy or glossy surfaces and helps to prevent flaking. It will also cover any print on the box. Leave overnight to dry thoroughly.

Cut a strip of paper long enough to go round the two long sides and one short side of the bus, and wide enough for the windows. Mark out the space for each window for younger children; older children can mark out their own. Cut the family photographs and stick one picture in each window space for the passengers. The child could be the driver. As an alternative to photographs you could cut pictures from magazines or use the child's own drawings. Glue the window strip around the bus, making sure that the driver is positioned on the front end of the box. Use card discs or bottle tops to make the wheels, glued to each corner of the bus. Paint the matchbox and glue it on to the front of the bus as the bonnet. Attach the calendar pad near the back of one side.

strip of paper

photographs or child's drawings

# ACTIVITY 12: DESK CALENDAR

**Materials needed**

Large Toblerone box; PVA glue; paint; calendar pad; assorted decorations (see below).

**What to do**

Paint the large Toblerone box with a mixture of two parts paint and one part PVA glue. Alternatively, spray it with gold spray paint (remember to do this in a well-ventilated area). Mount the calendar pad on a piece of coloured card or felt and glue to the centre of the box, as shown.

The space on either side can be decorated as you wish. You could use glitter and sequins for a sparkling calendar, or dried flowers and leaves for a more decorative one. Another idea would be to stick sporting pictures cut from magazines or cards, for someone who is interested in sport.

# ACTIVITY 13: CLOWN CALENDAR

**Materials needed**

Rectangle of card; coloured felt; pieces of wool; gummed paper shapes; glue; sequins; calendar pad.

**What to do**

Cut an oval of pink felt large enough for the clown's face. Make sure that there is enough room for the face and a pointed hat to fit on the card. Use brightly coloured felt and/or gummed paper to make the features and clothes. A large triangle of felt could be used for the clown's hat, small triangles of gummed paper for the ruff around his neck, triangles of felt for the eyes, with smaller circles of gummed paper in a different colour inside and, for the pupils, large sequins. Use a large rectangle for the mouth, just a little larger than the calendar pad, and a circle for the nose.

To assemble, position the face shape and the hat shape on the card, making sure that the point of the hat does not extend beyond the top of the card. Glue the face down, then glue a mass of tangled wool on either side for the hair. Glue the hat over the top of the wool. Now position the features and glue in place, then fix the calendar pad on to the mouth. Glue the triangles in

place to make the ruff, and finally decorate the ruff and the hat with large sequins and glitter. Fasten a loop of ribbon or coloured wool to the back of the calendar and hang it up.

# ACTIVITY 14: HOUSE CALENDAR

**Materials needed**

Rectangular cardboard box; coloured card or corrugated card; small cardboard tube; white paper; coloured papers; calendar pad; photographs of family members (head and shoulders) and full-length photograph of the child, or cut-out pictures from magazines or catalogues; paint; PVA glue.

**What to do**

Paint the box all over with a mixture of two parts paint to one part adhesive. Cut out coloured paper windows and a door of the appropriate size and glue these to the box when the paint is dry. To make the roof, cut a piece of card as long as the house and as wide as will make a suitably pitched roof. Score and fold along its length and bend into shape. Fold over each longest edge by 1 cm and glue these to the top of the box.

For the chimney cut a piece of cardboard tube about 10 cm long. Cut two 'V' shapes in the bottom to fit over the point of the roof and glue in place.

To personalise the house, each child can write the number of her own house on the door and glue the cut-out picture of herself standing at the side of it. The pictures of other family members can be placed in the windows, and the calendar pad can be stuck in one of the windows as well. Finally, decorate the walls of the house with flowers and shrubs to represent the garden.

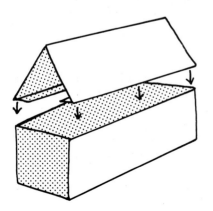

# ACTIVITY 15: PAPER SCULPTURE CALENDAR

**Materials needed**
White and coloured card; coloured foil; activity paper; length of wool or ribbon; glue; calendar pad.

**What to do**
To make this calendar the children will need to have had experience of cutting and handling paper and also learned some of the basic techniques of paper sculpture. Use white cartridge paper and let the children cut a variety of shapes. They can cut thick or thin strips or abstract shapes or they can draw around circular objects to get circles of different sizes. Encourage them to try looping strips of paper and making a concertina by folding the paper strip first one way and then the opposite way. They can make a spiral by winding a paper strip around a pencil and they can make a cone by cutting out a circle and then cutting a straight line from the edge to the centre and overlapping the cut edges.

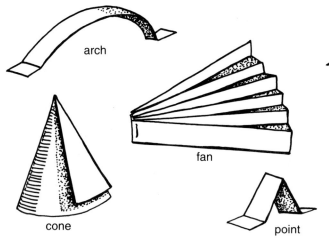

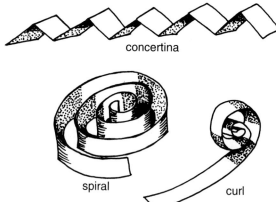

Give them the chance to experiment and create their own shapes and then make more shapes in coloured foil. When they have enough they can try out ways of positioning the shapes to make a pleasing design, and then glue them in place on a rectangle of card. Mount this on a larger piece of coloured card and glue the calendar pad underneath. Fasten a loop of wool to the back and hang in the usual way.

Once the children have had experience with the basic techniques, they can apply their skills to making faces. Cut out an oval shape for the face, make curled paper strips for hair, small cones for the eyes, a folded triangle for the nose and a curved mouth shape stuck just at the ends. Fringed paper strips can be glued above the eyes as eyebrows and around the chin for a beard, if desired. Glue the face on to a piece of card and position the calendar pad underneath the chin.

# ACTIVITY 16: PERPETUAL CALENDAR

**Materials needed**
Coloured card; white card; three spring-type clothes pegs; coloured wool or ribbon; glue.

**What to do**
Cut a piece of coloured card 35 cm × 30 cm: this will be the backing card. The days, months and dates can be written on a piece of white card, 12 cm wide × 50 cm long. Draw lines 1 cm apart down the length of the strip, then cut off twelve for the months, seven for the days and thirty-one for the dates.

The marking out of this calendar can be quite a challenging task for older children. For younger or less able children it may be preferable to draw the chart yourself and photocopy the sheet so that all they have to do is concentrate on filling in the information correctly. Once all the spaces have been marked out and all the information written in (using pencil first, in case of mistakes, and then felt-tip pen), glue the sheet to the backing card. The margin can be decorated if desired.

Fix a loop of wool to the back for hanging. Finally, clip one of the pegs to each section, to show the day, the date and the month.

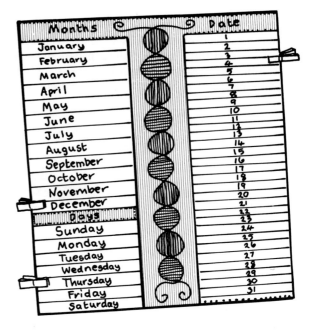

# ACTIVITY 17: COLLAGE CALENDAR

**Materials needed**
Rectangle of white card; larger rectangle of coloured card; assorted items for decoration (see below); ribbon or wool; calendar pad.

**What to do**
Using the smaller rectangle of card, decorate it in whatever way you wish. You could cover the whole area with patches of different seeds in a random manner or you could create a regular pattern by using the seeds to create lines of symmetry. Alternatively, you could arrange leaves and dried or pressed flowers on the card. Pasta, shells, sand, fleece and wool could be used in a similar way to make interesting calendar pictures.

When you have created the pattern or picture take a larger sheet of coloured card and mount the collage on this, leaving a border of 2 cm around the top three sides and a space of at least 8 cm at the bottom. In the middle of this space glue the calendar pad. A loop of ribbon or wool fixed to the top will enable the calendar to be hung.

# ACTIVITY 18: FROTTAGE CALENDAR

**Materials needed**
Card; assorted coloured paper; glue; calendar pad; wool or ribbon.

**What to do**
Decide on the pattern or scene you wish to create and break it down into component parts. The idea is to build up the picture, starting with the background. So if we decided to make a frottage picture showing a boat on the sea, we would need to make the horizon and the sky details first. Cut out a wavy horizon, making sure that it will fill the width of the card. Cut out a shape for the sun; the rays are optional. Next cut out a hull shape, a thin strip for the mast, triangular shapes for the sails and a small flag.

The cut-out pieces can be assembled on the card and glued in place. Finally, a second set of waves can be stuck over the bottom of the boat. Glue the card on to a larger card and fix the calendar pad on the bottom of this. Hang in the usual way with a loop of ribbon or wool on the back.

# ACTIVITY 19: HOT-AIR BALLOON CALENDAR

**Materials needed**
Card; paint; PVA glue; cardboard comb; string or wool; calendar pad; family group photograph or individual child photograph.

**What to do**
Cut out a large oval shape from the card to make the balloon. Paint it with a mixture of two parts paint and one part glue, then with a cardboard comb make criss-cross patterns on the surface. Cut a rectangular shape and paint this in the same way, this time making vertical and horizontal lines with the comb to represent the basket weave. When the paint is dry, assemble the balloon as shown by fixing two lengths of wool to the sides of the balloon near the bottom. Fix the basket to the free ends of the wool and make sure it hangs correctly.

Cut out the picture of the family group or child and glue or sellotape it to the back of the basket so that when you turn it over it looks as though the people are standing in the basket. Mount the calendar pad on a rectangle of card, and glue this to the bottom of the basket. Attach a loop of wool to the top of the balloon and hang it up.

*Back*

*Front*

# ACTIVITY 20: CYLINDER CALENDAR ▶

**Materials needed**
Cardboard tube; wool; paper; thin card; paint; glue; scraps of material; calendar pad.

**What to do**
Paint the cardboard tube flesh colour. Cut a strip of card 2.5 cm wide and long enough to go around the cardboard tube and stick out at the front as arms. Cut out two hand shapes from paper and glue these to the arms, as shown.

Now cut an oval-shaped piece of card for the face and draw on the features before gluing in place. Use lengths of wool or strips of paper for the hair. The figure can be decorated with scraps of material to make it look like an Indian, a fairy, a pirate, an angel or whatever you wish. The calendar pad is held in place by gluing it to a slightly larger piece of card and then gluing this to the hands.

# ACTIVITY 21: ANTIQUE METAL PLAQUE CALENDAR ▶

**Materials needed**
Large tin-foil pie plate; old ball-point pen or thick pencil; black shoe polish; black corrugated card; newspaper; pinking shears; cloth; calendar pad; glue.

**What to do**
Cut the rim from the pie plate with pinking shears to give an interesting zigzag edge. Rest the foil circle on several sheets of folded newspaper and draw over the design using a ball-point pen or a thick pencil. Encourage the children to work slowly and apply even

pressure to produce a well-defined line without puncturing the foil. When the pattern is completed turn the foil over to see the design in its raised form. Wipe over the raised side with black shoe polish and leave it to dry overnight.

Next day, polish the foil with a soft cloth to reveal the raised lines and some of the background. Mount the plaque on a larger circle of corrugated card to give a contrasting textured background. Finally, fix the calendar pad to the bottom and add a hanging loop at the top of the calendar.

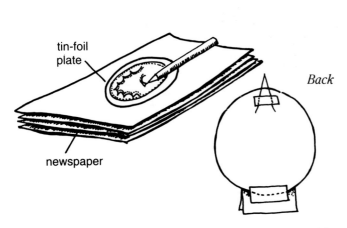

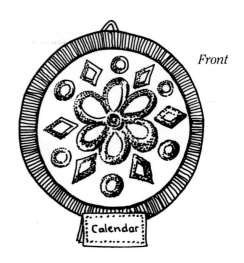

# ACTIVITY 22: SANTA'S SACK ADVENT CALENDAR

**Materials needed**
Large sheet of thin white card; strong brown paper bag; thin string, wool or ribbon; twenty-four small cardboard discs; wrapped sweets or small presents.

**What to do**
Draw a large picture of Father Christmas sitting in his sleigh on a sheet of thin card. Stick a strong paper bag on the bottom of the sleigh. Fold over the top of the bag to give it strength and shape.

Cut the string or ribbon into twenty-four pieces and tie one end to the sweets or small presents. Sellotape a small cardboard disc to the other end of each piece of string and number the discs from 1 to 24. Put the sweets or presents into the bag, leaving the discs hanging down on the outside. Each day the children can look for the appropriate string, remove it and the surprise will be discovered.

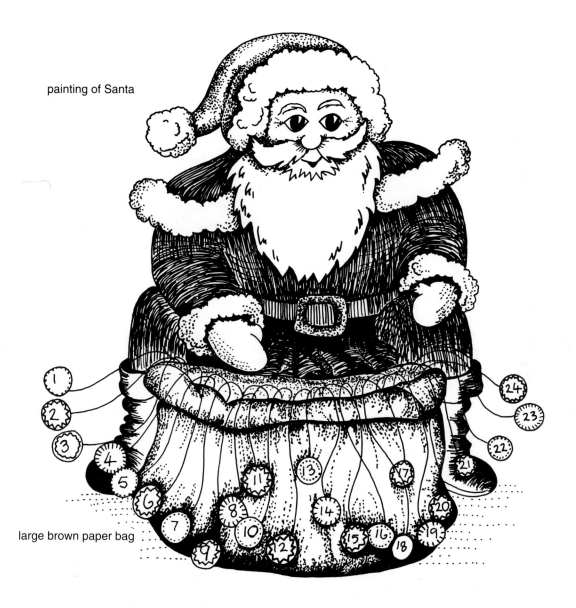

painting of Santa

large brown paper bag

25

# PRESENTS

## ACTIVITY 1: PAINTED WOODEN SPOON

**Materials needed**

Small new wooden spoon; gloss paint in assorted colours (e.g. Humbrol model paints); very fine paint brushes; turpentine or substitute; cloth; 30 cm of narrow ribbon in toning colour.

**What to do**

Paint simple designs of natural objects on the concave side of the spoon and the front of the handle. Suitable designs could include flowers, leaves, ears of barley or even small creatures such as a ladybird, a harvest mouse, a butterfly or a bird.

Keep a small amount of turpentine in a screw-top jar for cleaning brushes. If the children are working without direct supervision, instruct them not to breathe the fumes and keep the work area well ventilated.

To complete the decoration, make a small loop in the ribbon, held by a knot. Then position the loop at the back of the spoon near the top of the handle and tie the ribbon round the handle, finishing off at the front with a bow.

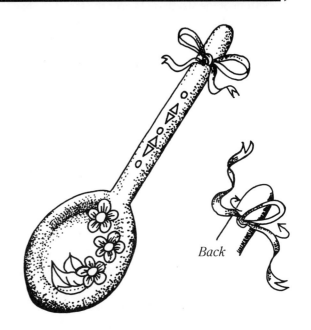

*Back*

## ACTIVITY 2: JAR OF CHOCOLATE CHERRIES

**Materials needed**

Small clear screw-top glass jar; red gingham or other red patterned cloth; narrow red ribbon; red rubber band; green, red and white paint (e.g. Humbrol model paints); fine paintbrush; Chocolate Cherries (see recipe p. 73); pinking shears.

**What to do**

Paint large circular cherries, evenly spaced, all round the outside of the jar. Leave to dry thoroughly before adding a couple of green leaves to the top of each cherry and a small dot of white, as the shine, on each red circle.

Fill the jar with the homemade cherries. Before fastening the lid, measure its diameter and then draw a circle on the red cloth at least 7 cm larger in diameter than the lid. Pinking shears will give a decorative edge to the cloth. Put the lid on the jar, place the cloth circle over it and fix in place with the rubber band. Finally, tie the red ribbon over the band and secure with a decorative bow.

26

# ACTIVITY 3: SEASONAL BOOKMARK

**Materials needed**
Blue or yellow acetate sheet; PVA glue; red and green art paper; 20 cm each of red and green narrow silk ribbon.

**What to do**
Cut a strip of acetate 5 cm × 15 cm and cut a point at one end. Cut out two holly leaves from green art paper and three large berries from the red paper. These can be arranged on the acetate strip and stuck down with a little PVA glue. To finish off the bookmark, use a hole punch to make a hole in the straight end of the acetate and thread through the two ribbons, tying or looping them together.

# ACTIVITY 4: A WRITING SET

**Materials needed**
White A3 cartridge paper; PVA glue; paint in assorted colours; white A4 paper; small envelopes; scraps of card; thick paintbrushes; coloured paper.

**What to do**
First decorate the paper that is to be used for the folder. Use two or three different colours of paint (each mixed two parts paint to one part glue) and paint stripes thickly over the whole surface of the A3 paper, leaving no spaces. Next make a comb for the pattern work by cutting rough zigzags on one edge of a piece of tough card. Use this to make a wavy line design through the paint stripes, going at right angles to the original lines and drawing the colours into each other. Leave it to dry overnight until the painted design is firm and 'plastic' to the touch. It is now ready to be made into a folder.

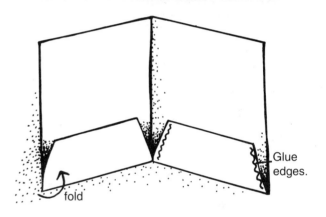

fold

Glue edges.

Add a strip of coloured paper (3 cm × 15 cm) as a stamp pocket, glued along the bottom and sides. You can choose a colour that tones with one in the paint design. Cut about twelve sheets of A4 paper in half lengthways and put these in one of the pockets as writing paper, then put six envelopes in the other side.

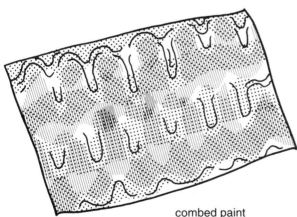

combed paint

Fold the decorated paper in half with a firm crease to make an A4-size booklet, then open it out and fold the bottom upwards, as shown, to make the pockets. Trim narrow triangles off the edges and centre of this fold so that the folder will close easily. Stick the edges down with a little glue.

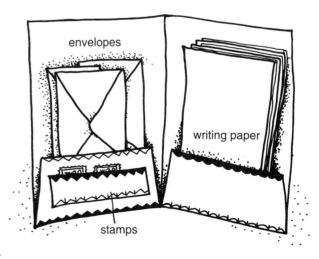

envelopes

writing paper

stamps

# ACTIVITY 5: PRESSED-FLOWER GARDENING FOLDER

## Materials needed

Coloured A4 card; small pieces of art paper; transparent Fablon or Contact; glue; three sheets A4 white paper; two or three packets of seeds; three or four plant labels; assorted wild or garden flowers; thick newspaper.

## What to do

First of all you will need to prepare the pressed flowers earlier in the term to let them dry out. Choose varieties of small flowers such as buttercup, pansy, dianthus and those with flat petals. Flowers with composite heads such as dandelions and those with fine, narrow petals like daisies are not suitable as they don't dry out attractively. For the folder you will need about six flowers and six leaves or some grasses. Lay them flat and spaced out between sheets of folded newspaper. Place about 1 cm thickness of newspaper between each layer of flowers and put the whole wad under a seat or other weight for a few weeks until the flowers and leaves have dried out. You can of course use a flower press if one is available.

The folder is made by folding the card in half to A5 size. Make a good crease by drawing the line first with a pencil and then scoring it lightly with scissors and a ruler. To make the pockets for the seed packets, cut two pieces of coloured art paper, 13 cm × 4 cm, and with a thin line of glue fix them inside the folder on the left-hand side, as shown.

Turn the folder over so that the outside is uppermost and arrange the dried flowers in a pattern, mostly on the front but with a small motif on the back too. The decorated folder can now be covered with a transparent sticky-backed plastic such as Fablon. Cut a piece of plastic about 2 cm larger than the A4 card so that the excess can be folded over to the inside. Finish the plastic cover neatly with mitred corners and press over the flowers to give a good contact and to allow the colour to show through well.

Use the white paper to make a notepad of about six sheets, slightly smaller than A5 size. Fix this inside the folder with three neatly placed staples. Add two or three packets of seeds and some plant labels to complete the gift.

To personalise it, the name of the recipient could be made by cutting out letters from art paper and sticking them lightly on the front cover before adding the Fablon.

newspaper

*Back*     *Front*

Fablon

Dad

glue

mitred corners    seed packet pockets

Pansy

Brown's Seeds   Mr. Foster

Notes

paper pad

*Inside of folder*

# ACTIVITY 6: LAVENDER BAGS

**Materials needed**
Colourful printed cotton fabric (12 cm × 30 cm); sewing thread and needle; narrow silk ribbon; large dessertspoonful of lavender flowers; lavender essence; orris root powder.

**What to do**
To make the bag, fold the fabric in half along its length and sew a fine hem about 1 cm from each side to form a bag. Iron this seam flat, then fold the top of the bag back 3 cm and press it flat. This can now be hemmed neatly to complete the bag.

Lavender can be bought from garden centres or herbalists at about £2 for half a kilogram, which is enough to make about thirty small bags of this size. If you are making several bags prepare all the lavender at once. Mix three teaspoons of orris root powder with the lavender and add a few drops of lavender essence if the scent is not strong enough on its own. Now all you need to do is put a large dessertspoonful in each bag and finish off by tying the neck of the bag with a coloured ribbon.

# ACTIVITY 7: SEED BROOCH

**Materials needed**
Circle of card (5 cm diameter); circle of brown felt (same size); small safety pin; half a hazelnut shell; lentils; sunflower seeds or pumpkin seeds; clear nail varnish; Copydex adhesive.

**What to do**
Select half of a hazelnut shell which is evenly broken and a good round shape. Cover the card circle with a good depth of Copydex and embed the hazelnut shell in the centre, with the outside upwards. Use the pumpkin or sunflower seeds for the petals of the flower shape, resting half their length on the glue bed to give them a secure base. If you use pumpkin seeds you will need fewer of them as they are very large. Next dab a little more glue over the inner ends of the petals and sprinkle on the lentils around the base of the hazelnut.

Leave the sculpture to dry thoroughly then attach the felt backing circle and the safety pin as shown, using Copydex again. When this is dry add a final touch with a light coat of clear nail varnish over the seeds to highlight the natural colour and give a protective sheen.

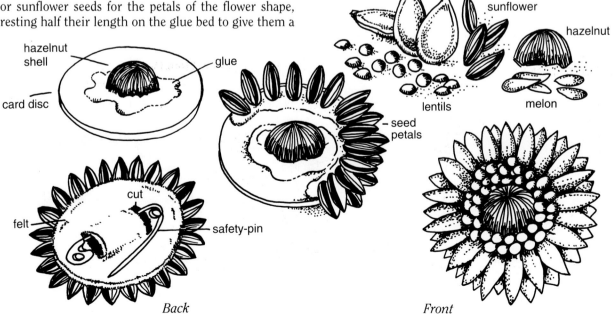

29

# ACTIVITY 8: DESIGNER BROOCHES

**Materials needed**

Salt dough (2 cups flour, 1 cup salt, 1 cup water); poster paints; clear nail varnish or PVA glue; Copydex adhesive; safety pins; small pieces of card.

**What to do**

To make the dough, mix the dry ingredients together then add as much of the water as you need to make a pliable dough. Knead this well. Each brooch can be made from a piece the size of a walnut. Simple shapes like those shown are most suitable for the comfort of the wearer and the durability of the brooch. Try to avoid too many small pieces protruding from the main body of

the brooch as they are apt to break off easily. To ensure good joins if you need to add pieces, use a little water or roughen the surfaces to be joined.

Put the collection of brooches on a flat baking tray and bake them at 160°C/325°F/gas mark 3 for about 30 minutes, then leave them to cool thoroughly before going on to the next stage. They can now be painted with poster paints and then given a sheen with a coat of nail varnish or PVA glue. Gloss different coloured areas separately to avoid the possibility of colours merging. Finally add the fastener by gluing a safety pin to the back with a small circle of card and Copydex adhesive.

# ACTIVITY 9: STONE PAPER WEIGHTS

**Materials needed**

Smooth round stones (adult palm size); gloss paints in assorted colours; turpentine or substitute; old cloth; small paint brush.

**What to do**

Wash the stones thoroughly before starting then select those which sit well on a surface and have a good smooth upper face to paint on. For the paint you can provide either a small palette to hold paint from larger pots or small pots of Humbrol enamels. The brush will

need to be cleaned between colours so keep a screw-top jar with just a little turps in it on the work surface and an old cloth to wipe the brushes on. If the children are working without direct supervision, as older ones can do, instruct them not to breathe the fumes and keep the work area well ventilated at all times. The children should wash their hands after working with the paints.

This gift is very easy to make. All you need to do is paint a simple design or picture on the top surface of the stone, let it dry and, if you feel it needs a gloss, add a coat of clear nail varnish, polyurethane varnish or PVA glue.

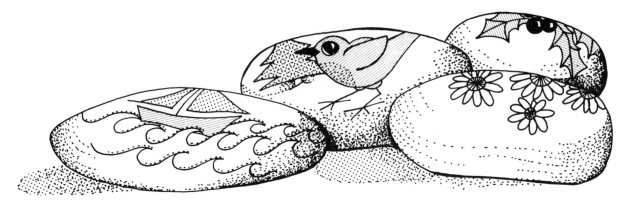

# ACTIVITY 10: DESIGNER MIRROR

## Materials needed
Small handbag mirror; Copydex adhesive; Polyfilla; stiff card (10 cm × 15 cm and 10 cm × 10 cm); assorted small decorations (see below).

## What to do
Prepare the mount first by sticking the small piece of card to the back of the larger piece, as shown, to act as the stand. Next glue the mirror to the centre of the front, using Copydex. Mix up the Polyfilla and paste it thickly round the outside of the mirror on the card frame. You will need to lie the mirror flat to do this. You might also cover the mirror with a piece of paper to protect it; the paper can be removed when the decorations have been stuck on.

For the decoration you could use small shells, coloured beads, seeds, pasta shapes or anything else you choose. Sometimes a neat row of similar-sized shells can be pleasing in its simplicity. However, the artist may find a combination of glitter, pasta shells and buttons to be most attractive. Ask the children to think carefully about their selection, considering texture, shape and colour. The items are just pressed gently into the polyfilla to secure them. Leave to dry thoroughly. The frame can be left as it is or it could be varnished, painted or sprayed with gold spray paint. To spray it, cover the mirror and place the frame on newspaper in a well-ventilated area, then spray carefully. This should be done by an adult or under adult supervision.

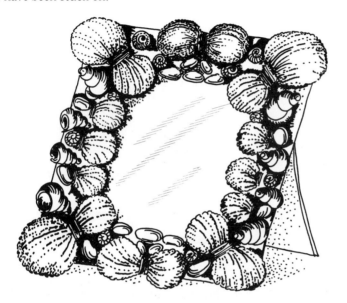

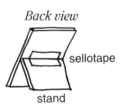

*Back view*

sellotape

stand

# ACTIVITY 11: TINY CHRISTMAS STOCKING

## Materials needed
Felt in assorted colours; sequins and beads; narrow ribbon; Copydex adhesive; stapler.

## What to do
Cut out two stocking shapes from the felt, about 15 cm long and 8 cm across at the widest point. The toe of the stocking should point downwards. Glue the two sides together along a narrow strip, using Copydex. Make a hanging loop by looping some ribbon and tying a knot to secure it, then tying a bow on the knot. Staple this to the top corner of the stocking.

You can now decorate the stocking with small cut-out felt motifs such as stars, trees or baubles. These can be stuck on with a little Copydex. Beads or sequins can also be added. A narrow cuff of white felt or cotton wool looks attractive too; this will need to be attached before the hanging loop.

This miniature stocking can be used as a container for a small gift such as a comb, a pen, some sweets or a hankie.

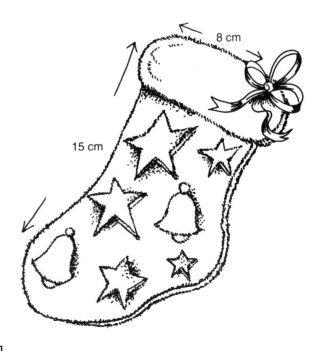

8 cm

15 cm

31

# ACTIVITY 12: DINNER CANDLE LAMP

**Materials needed**

Medium-size glass jar; white or yellow candle; Blu-tack; gold and silver enamel paint, such as Humbrol; old washing-up bowl; water; old paintbrush; turpentine; old cloth; newspaper.

**What to do**

First of all prepare the marbling. Half fill the bowl with cold water and then, using the end of the brush, drop a little of the gold paint on to the surface of the water. This should spread over the surface in a coiled pattern. Now drop on some silver paint, then more gold, until the surface of the water is covered with separated and swirled rivers of paint. The bottom of the jar can now be dipped in the paint to a depth of about 4 cm and then lifted out straight away. The swirled paint pattern should have transferred to the bottom of the jar. Leave it to dry for several hours, standing the jar on its neck on newspaper. The neck of the jar can then be dipped in the same way; you will need to replenish the paint before dipping. The brush can be cleaned in a little turpentine; make sure this is done in a well-ventilated area.

Cut the candle to a length about 5 cm below the top of the jar. Fix a large ball of Blu-tack in the bottom of the jar and push the candle into it.

When the candle is lit, the jar can become quite hot so care must be taken when handling.

# ACTIVITY 13: WOODEN KEY TIDY

**Materials needed**

A piece of softwood (15 cm × 12 cm × 2 cm), such as skirting board offcut; sandpaper; 2 brass straight hooks; 2 small curtain eyelets; 30 cm narrow silk ribbon; family photograph; wood varnish; paintbrush; turpentine; old cloth; Copydex adhesive.

**What to do**

Prepare the wood by sanding it carefully and then put on one or two coats of clear or coloured varnish. Clean the brush with turpentine. The work area must be well

ventilated when turps and varnish are used and hands must be washed carefully afterwards.

Fix the screw eyelets in the sides of the wood, as shown, about 2 cm from the top. Next fix the large brass hooks to the front of the wood, to hold the keys.

If you wish to personalise the gift, choose a photograph which the recipient of the gift would like and glue this to the top part of the front, above the key hooks. The ribbon can now be tied to the side hooks to make a colourful hanger to complete the key holder.

curtain eyelet

brass hooks

# ACTIVITY 14: TRINKET TUB

**Materials needed**
Cylindrical food container with plastic lid (e.g. cocoa tin); pictures cut from postcards, greetings cards or photographs, or postage stamps; Copydex adhesive; rosette gift bow (same colour as plastic lid); clear Fablon or clear polyurethane varnish.

**What to do**
Begin by cutting out a selection of small pictures; more can be cut as they are needed. Choose pictures on good quality paper like postcards, thicker wrapping paper, calendars or family photographs. Make sure the surface of the container is free from bumps and remains of labels. Using Copydex, which is a quick-drying adhesive, start to stick on the pictures, slightly overlapping each one to give complete coverage. Smooth over each picture to get rid of any air bubbles. More pictures can be cut out as the job proceeds. Don't overlap the top or the bottom of the cylinder, just touch the edges with the pictures then a neater finish will result.

Covering the finished montage is the next step and there are two methods of doing this. The first is to cover the cylinder with clear Fablon. Measure the depth and the circumference of the cylinder and allow a half centimetre overlap on the latter to give a good join. The Fablon should be laid on a surface and the cylinder rolled on to it, then carefully smoothed to remove all bubbles. Press well over the plastic so that the colours of the picture show through it.

Alternatively, the surface can be varnished with a good clear varnish. This is more time consuming but effective and suitable for older children. At least six coats are needed for a good lacquered effect and each coat should be lightly sanded when dry, apart from the last one. (If using varnish make sure the area is well ventilated.)

To complete the gift, stick the ribbon on the plastic lid.

cut-out pictures

# ACTIVITY 15: GEOMETRIC PICTURE FRAME

**Materials needed**
Corrugated card; small pasta shapes; Copydex adhesive; stiff card; photograph; gold spray paint.

**What to do**
Cut two pieces of stiff card, each 18 cm × 15 cm. In one piece cut a hole in the centre slightly smaller than your photograph. Glue the outside edges of both pieces together on three sides, leaving one side open to take the photograph. Make a stand from a piece of card (15 cm × 15 cm) and sellotape it to the back, as shown.

Now cut a selection of small geometric shapes from the corrugated card and arrange these around the front of the frame in a rectangular pattern, tessellating shapes if possible. Glue these in place and add a row of small pasta shapes round the central hole to give an attractive edging. It is advisable to put in a blank sheet of paper instead of the photo in case the glue goes over the edge. Next spray the front and sides of the frame with gold spray paint. An adult or older child under supervision should do this in a well-ventilated area. Remove the blank paper and slip in the photograph.

# ACTIVITY 16: BARBECUE CANDLE ▶

**Materials needed**
Newclay (or other self-hardening clay); modelling tools; paint; PVA glue; paintbrushes; small nightlight candle.

**What to do**
Make the candle shell by taking a ball of modelling clay about the size of a small apple to make a thumb pot.

Hold the clay cupped in the palm of the left hand and push the thumb of the right hand into it. Then, holding the clay with thumb and forefinger, turn the ball round, pressing the clay gently to form a hollowed vessel with the walls about 1 cm thick. It needs to be about 5 cm taller than the nightlight. Make sure that the nightlight will fit into the vessel.

Stand it on a flat surface to flatten the base and smooth out and straighten the sides. It can then be decorated with patterns made by modelling tools. Small holes can be made near the top of the pot to allow the light to shine through. To do this, support the inside of the vessel with the fingers and thumb of one hand and use a small hollow item such as a metal tube to push the clay through to the fingers. Smooth the edges with a little water. Allow the clay to dry thoroughly and brush with any hardening liquids recommended. The hardener usually makes a significant difference to the texture and lasting properties.

The vessel can now be decorated by spraying with gold paint or painting with a mixture of PVA glue and paint in equal quantities. Alternatively, it could be covered with glue and rolled in glitter or sand to give an unusual texture. Stand the nightlight in the vessel to complete the gift.

# ACTIVITY 17: MARBLED CANDLESTICK ▶

**Materials needed**
Glass bottle with a neck large enough to hold a candle; coloured candle; gloss paints or Humbrol paints; old washing-up bowl; turpentine; water; old cloth; thin paintbrush; rubber gloves.

**What to do**
Wash and dry the bottle carefully then prepare the paints. Choose colours that tone with the colour of the glass and ones that the recipient will like. Half fill the bowl with cold water and drop on blobs of paint all over the surface. They should begin to move and swirl together; the tip of a brush can be used to draw the colours into lines and spirals. When the surface is covered, carefully lie the bottle on its side and, holding the neck, draw it across the surface of the water, turning it round as you do so. The glass will take up the pattern of the paint. Depending on the size of the bottle, you may need to re-apply the paint to the water and repeat the process. However, with a coloured bottle a partial covering of paint can look very effective.

Use rubber gloves to handle the bottle so that the hands don't get covered in paint and try not to cover the bottom of the bottle as that makes drying difficult. Remember to work in a well-ventilated area because

gloss paint gives off a certain amount of fumes. The brush can be cleaned in turpentine, which is best kept in a screw-top jar and used by adults only.

Allow the paint to dry thoroughly before inserting the candle.

# ACTIVITY 18: POT POURRI PARCELS

**Materials needed**

Assorted pieces of fabric and net in toning colours; velvet ribbons; pinking shears; pot-pourri; rubber bands.

**What to do**

For each parcel cut out two circles of fabric using pinking shears, one in net (22 cm diameter) and one in fabric (20 cm diameter). Use colours that will go well together. You will need a 30 cm piece of velvet ribbon for each parcel. Lay the smaller circle on a work surface with the net on top of it and put a good handful of pot-pourri in the centre. Gather up the circles into a posy bag and secure the top with a rubber band. Open out the gathers and finish off by tying the velvet ribbon in a bow around the neck.

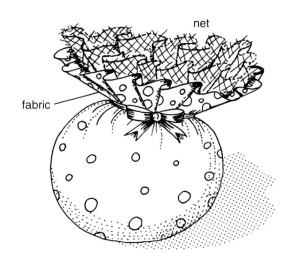

# ACTIVITY 19: MR WOBBLE TOY

**Materials needed**

Plaster of Paris; plastic funnel; water; round-bottomed plastic drinks bottle; Copydex adhesive; scraps of wool and felt, paper and other items for decoration.

**What to do**

Make up the plaster of Paris as directed and pour it into the bottom of the bottle to a depth of about 6 cm, using a funnel. Try not to get any plaster on the rest of the bottle. Once it is dry the bottom can be stripped off the bottle, as shown. The bottle will now be wobbly, so put it in a heavy bowl or other container to make it easier to work on. Test the wobble first.

The bottle can be decorated as any character you wish, using felt, wool, paper curls and any other materials. A circle of card may be used as a base for the face; fix it with Copydex adhesive which is very quick drying and particularly suitable for vertical surfaces. Older children should be able to cut out the felt and other fabrics themselves, but younger ones may need help.

This makes an appealing present for young children.

# ACTIVITY 20: GLITTERING GIFT BOX

**Materials needed**

Small shoe box (child's size); gold spray paint; PVA glue; gold glitter; assorted colours of ready-mixed paint; small objects for printing.

**What to do**

Spray the box and the lid all over, on the outside only, with gold spray paint and let it dry thoroughly. Remember to do this in a well-ventilated area to avoid breathing in the fumes.

To decorate the gold box you can print on a design using small scrap items such as Smartie tube lids, cotton reels, pencil ends and so on. For this purpose the printing medium is a mixture of one part PVA glue and one part ready-mixed paint. Print the design on the gold surface and before it dries sprinkle a little gold glitter on each motif to add a sparkle. This should stick well to the

glue in the paint mixture. Allow the box to dry then put a scrunched up sheet of tissue paper, in an appropriate colour, inside the box to hold the gift.

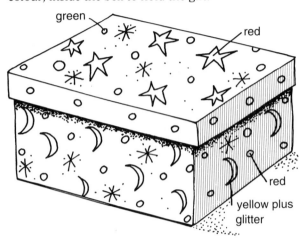

green
red
red
yellow plus glitter

# ACTIVITY 21: PIGGY BANK

**Materials needed**

Balloon; newspaper; PVA glue; four corks; large bottle top; pipe-cleaner; ready-mixed paint; card; polyurethane clear varnish; paintbrushes; turpentine; old cloths.

**What to do**

Blow up the balloon and secure it. Tear the newspaper into strips about $2\,\text{cm} \times 10\,\text{cm}$. Paste the strips individually with glue and stick them over the balloon to give total cover. This layer can be left to dry thoroughly and then six more layers added, each time pasting the paper strips at right angles to the last one to give strength. Be sure to let each layer dry before doing the next.

To add the features, use masking tape to fix four corks in place as legs and a bottle top as the nose. Cut out two large triangles of card for ears and use the tape to fix these and also the pipe cleaner tail. You will now need to paste on two more layers of newspaper to cover the

features and fix them securely to the body. The children will enjoy popping the balloon at this stage by sticking a pin through the paper layers.

When the final layers are dry, cut a slit in the top for the money and make an emptying hole in the bottom. To do this, find a plastic bottle top of a suitable size and use it as a template to draw the hole. Cut out the hole slightly smaller and push in the top as a stopper.

To colour the pig, start off with a coat of white emulsion and then paint a chosen colour scheme using ready-mixed watercolour paint. Finish off with a coat of clear varnish to give a very durable product. The children can of course choose variations on the spherical theme and make fish, clowns' heads, footballs or even a giant apple money box.

Remember to keep turpentine covered and out of the reach of younger children. Children should also wash their hands carefully after cleaning brushes with turps and varnish on them.

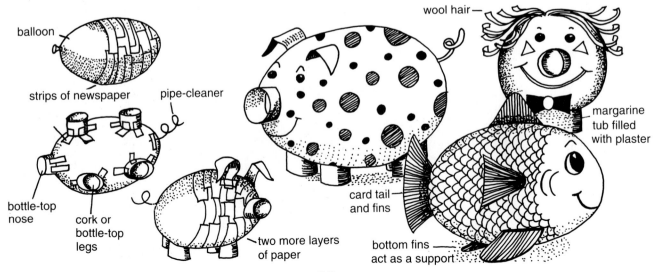

balloon

strips of newspaper    pipe-cleaner

bottle-top nose

cork or bottle-top legs

two more layers of paper

wool hair

margarine tub filled with plaster

card tail and fins

bottom fins act as a support

# ACTIVITY 22: DECORATED PAPER BOWL

**Materials needed**

Pottery bowl as a mould; clingfilm; white paper; PVA glue; pictures cut out from old postcards, etc.

**What to do**

Making sure that the bowl has a clean, dry surface, cover it completely with cling film and press this on to the surface. Cut the paper into strips about 2 cm × 10 cm, paste them with glue and cover the inside surface of the bowl with about eight layers of paper, letting each layer dry before adding the next. A good edge can be achieved by curving the layers slightly over the edge of the bowl as they are glued on. When the layers are dry, the paper bowl can be removed from its mould and the outside curve of the rim can be trimmed with scissors.

To decorate the bowl, cut out plenty of small pictures from thick wrapping paper, postcards or photographs, choosing pictures that are appropriate for the recipient of the gift. Stick the pictures on, slightly overlapping, until the whole surface is covered. For ease of handling start with the inside surfaces and let this dry, then turn it over and complete the back of the bowl. Again, let this dry thoroughly then give the bowl a durable finish with a coat of PVA glue, which will be clear when dry, or polyurethane varnish for a glossy surface.

layers of paper
curved over rim

paper strips

bowl covered
in cling film

finished bowl covered in
cut-out paper flower pictures

# ACTIVITY 23: NAME PLATES

**Materials needed**

Salt dough (2 cups plain flour, 1 cup salt, 1 tablespoon oil, water to mix); ready-mixed paints; polyurethane varnish; turpentine; old cloths; paintbrushes.

**What to do**

Mix the flour, salt, oil and a little water together in a bowl until you have a ball of dough, then turn it out on to a floured surface and knead until it is pliable.

Now you can make a variety of shapes of name plates, based on the ideas shown here. Long sausages of dough can be plaited together to edge an oval plaque or two sausages can be twisted together. Dough can be rolled

and cut to shape with a knife. Shapes can be cut with pastry cutters and stuck on to a dough base with a touch of water. Patterns can be pressed into the dough with old spoons, knives or pencils. Letters can be cut out of rolled pastry or formed from thin sausages. To make a hanger for the name plate, stick a paper clip into the top edge before baking.

To harden the dough, put the shaped name plate on a piece of baking foil on a tray and bake in a pre-heated oven (160°C/325°F/gas mark 3) for about an hour. Let the dough cool before decorating it with ready-mixed paint and finishing off with a coat of varnish. Remember safety measures when using varnish and turpentine.

# ROOM AND TREE DECORATIONS

## ACTIVITY 1: RIBBON ROSETTES

**Materials needed**

Shiny parcel ribbon (the kind that sticks to itself when moistened).

**What to do**

Cut the parcel ribbon into lengths of 21 cm. This will give a loop of 10 cm, allowing for an overlap of 1 cm. Make a loop by moistening one end and curving it over to join on to the other end. Position the join in the middle of the loop and stick it to the opposite side of the loop to create two smaller loops of equal size, as shown. Make several loops in this way.

To assemble the rosette, take two loops and position them at right angles to each other. Moisten the centre and stick them together to make a cross. Add more loops to fill in the spaces. Obviously the more loops you add the fuller will be the rosette. Make sure you balance the number of loops on each side. Finally make a loop of thin parcel ribbon, thread it through one of the loops of the rosette and stick the ends together. The finished rosette can be hung on the tree.

## ACTIVITY 2: WINDOW FAN

**Materials needed**

Roll of paper or coloured foil; 2 elastic bands; stapler; double-sided sticky tape.

**What to do**

Choose the window you wish to decorate. You need a roll of paper half the width of the window, so if the window is 60 cm wide the width of the paper will need to be 30 cm. Rolls of lining paper are useful and inexpensive. Start from one end of the roll and fold the paper in 3 cm concertina folds, making the pleats crisp and even. Keep fitting the paper to the window, and

when the fan of paper opens to a full semi-circle, cut it off the roll. Put an elastic band around each end of the paper to hold the pleats in place.

Use scissors to make simple straight cuts through three or four layers of paper at a time and carry on cutting until you have cut a pattern through all the layers. Staple through all the pleats at one end of the fan, then open it out carefully. Hold it in place against the window with sticky tabs or double-sided tape. Finally dab the window with white paint to represent snowflakes. Fans made from coloured foil give the classroom a very festive appearance.

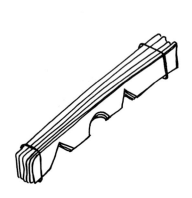 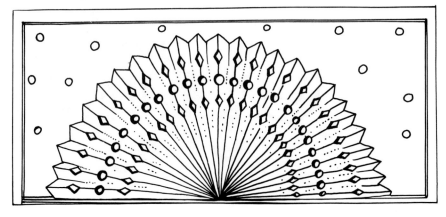

# ACTIVITY 3: WINTER SCENE ▶

**Materials needed**

Cereal packet; selection of old Christmas cards; tin foil; small cardboard boxes; plasticene; pieces of twig; small fir cones; cotton wool; glitter.

**What to do**

Cut a large empty cereal packet in half to make a tray. Cut out a selection of winter scenes from old Christmas cards and glue them round three sides, overlapping them to create a background scene. Cover two or three smaller boxes with white paper and glue them to the base, putting the tallest boxes at the back. Cut out pictures of churches and houses from Christmas cards and glue them to the boxes. Cover the base of the tray with cotton wool to represent snow, and cut a pond shape from tin foil. Press small pieces of twig into plasticene for trees, or use fir cones.

Cut out or draw your own pictures of children playing in the snow, and assemble all the features in the scene. You could make a snowman from two cotton wool balls glued one on top of the other; draw in the features using a black felt-tip pen, use a bottle top for a hat and a strip of coloured felt or crêpe paper for a scarf. Finally sprinkle a little glitter over the scene.

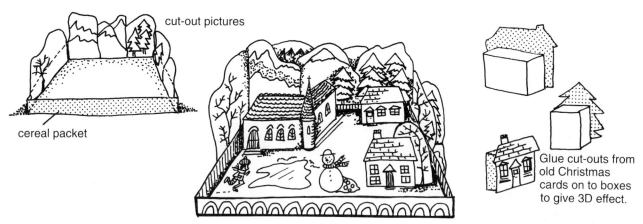

cut-out pictures

cereal packet

Glue cut-outs from old Christmas cards on to boxes to give 3D effect.

# ACTIVITY 4: SNOW BIRD MOBILE ▶

**Materials needed**

White cartridge paper; Copydex adhesive; silver ribbon; silver foil; glitter; sequins; silver metallic thread.

**What to do**

Cut out a bird shape from cartridge paper. Take a rectangle of paper 30 cm × 20 cm and fold it down the middle of the longest side. With the fold at the top, draw a wavy design on one side and cut off the lower part through both layers: this will be the bird's tail.

Cut out strips of white paper and curl them or fold into concertina shapes to represent feathers. Stick them to the tail, along with strips of silver foil and silver ribbon. You can also add sequins and glitter. Staple the tail in place. Next make a small hole in the middle of the bird's back and thread silver metallic thread through it to enable the snowbird to be hung. Decorate the head and body with silver sequins, and add a piece of Blu-tack at the bottom to help balance the body and tail.

Several snowbirds could be displayed with giant snowflakes hung from the ceiling.

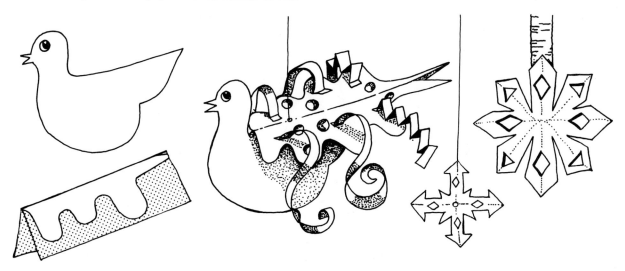

39

# ACTIVITY 5: FATHER CHRISTMAS MOBILE

**Materials needed**
Pink card; red felt; cotton wool; glue; crêpe paper or ribbon.

**What to do**
Cut an oval or a round shape from the pink card to make the face. Cut a triangle shape from the card and fold vertically from the top point: this is for the nose. Stick the nose in the centre of the face shape. Draw in the eyes and the mouth with felt-tip pen. Make a moustache and a beard from cotton wool and glue on.

Fix a strip of cotton wool around the top of the face for the hair. Cut out a large triangle of red felt for the hat and glue it to the top of the head. Staple a strip of crêpe paper or ribbon to the point of the hat so that the mobile can be hung, then cover the staple with a ball of cotton wool.

# ACTIVITY 6: CHRISTMAS PINATA

**Materials needed**
Balloon; Vaseline; wallpaper paste; newspapers; bucket; cotton wool; paints; glue.

**What to do**
Mix the wallpaper paste and soak strips of newspaper in it. Blow up the balloon, tie it and cover it all over with Vaseline. Then cover the balloon with the paste-soaked strips of newspaper, leaving a small area free around the neck of the balloon. Leave to dry thoroughly. When it is dry, pop the balloon and remove it.

With the hole at the top, paint a Father Christmas face on the pinata shape and glue on a cotton wool beard and moustache. Put a few unbreakable toys and some sweets inside the shape and attach ribbons to the top with glue to cover the hole and to make a hanging loop.

Hang the pinata in a suitable place, then blindfold the children and give each one a roll of newspaper. The object is to try to knock the pinata to the ground and find the surprise presents.

paper strips soaked
in wallpaper paste

# ACTIVITY 7: KISSING BUNCH

**Materials needed**
Two wire coat-hangers; green garden twine; pieces of holly, laurel and ivy; small unbreakable tree baubles; mistletoe; red or tartan ribbon.

**What to do**
Pull the coat-hangers into a circular shape and slide one inside the other to create a ball, with the hooks together at the top. Bind them together with garden twine. Using more twine, tie bunches of evergreens on to the wire hoops until the entire ball is covered. You may need to wear thick gardening gloves and be especially careful when handling holly. Add a few baubles, and in the centre of the bunch hang a piece of fresh mistletoe. The coat-hanger hooks can be covered with red or tartan ribbon and used to hang the Kissing Bunch from the ceiling. Tie a few pieces of ribbon to the bottom for added effect.

two
wire coat-hangers

# ACTIVITY 8: LARGE CHRISTMAS BAUBLES

**Materials needed**
Large sheets of white paper; wax crayons and water-based paints or Copydex adhesive and powder paints; coloured foil; doilies; old Christmas cards; glue; glitter; sequins.

**What to do**
Let the children draw very large Christmas bauble shapes on the paper; if necessary, draw the outline yourself for younger children. They can then paint and decorate them as they wish.

One idea is to use the wax-resist method. The children draw patterns using thick wax crayons, then paint over the top of this with water-based paints. A similar effect can be achieved by trailing Copydex adhesive from a squeezy bottle over the sheet of paper. Leave it to dry, then sprinkle coloured powder paint over the surface. Next wet the surface with a fine spray of water until the paint is wet and runs together. Leave the whole thing to dry, then very carefully peel off the trails of Copydex to reveal a pattern of white trailing lines, where the paint has not reached. If the centre is to be decorated, use a gold or silver doily with a picture cut out from an old Christmas card. Alternatively, cut snowflakes from different coloured foil and sprinkle with glitter or sequins.

Cut out the baubles and pin or Blu-tack them to the wall and link them together around the room with a deep fringe of dark green crêpe paper.

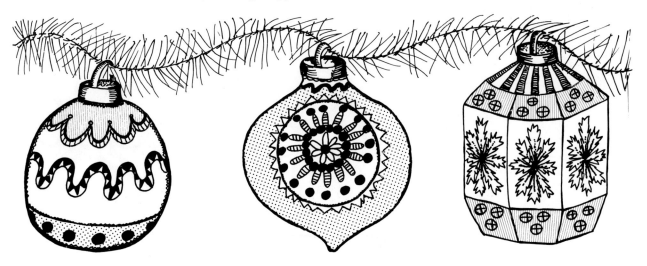

41

# ACTIVITY 9: STARRY CHANDELIERS

## Materials needed
White or coloured card; gold, silver and coloured foil paper; coloured cellophane; sequins, glitter; glue; wool or twine.

## What to do
Cut pieces of card 40 cm × 15 cm and form into cylinders. Glue the edges together. Cut card strips, 3 cm wide but of varying lengths. The strips can be decorated on both sides with sequins and glitter, stars cut from foil paper and cellophane strips curled, scrunched or tied into bows. Staple or glue the decorations on to each strip to curve over in an arch.

To hang the cylinder, make two holes opposite each other near the top rim; thread wool or twine through and tie in a loop.

Hang the cylinders close to each other but at different levels. The decoration on both sides of the arched strips will ensure that the chandeliers look good from any level.

hanging loop

strip stapled to inside of top rim

15 cm

# ACTIVITY 10: QUILLING STARS

## Materials needed
Thin strips of paper, approximately 2 cm wide. (A guillotine will produce strips quickly. You can use coloured activity paper or coloured foil. The double-sided foil is slightly thicker and keeps its shape well.) You will also need glue, needle and thread.

## What to do
Use the strips of paper to make a variety of shapes: squares, circles, spirals, triangles and so on (as for the Quilling Calendar on p. 17).

If you use the glue sparingly, the joints will dry

faster, but make sure there is enough glue to hold the shape together. Give the children the opportunity to experiment by positioning the shapes together first, in order to create designs they like. Try to ensure that the designs they produce are balanced and symmetrical. The children will have to be careful to apply the glue in the correct places on the curved surfaces to ensure that the individual shapes join where they are supposed to. Leave until the glue is fully dry, then, by holding the star between finger and thumb, test for balance. Pass a needle and thread through a strip at the top of the star and make a loop to enable it to be hung.

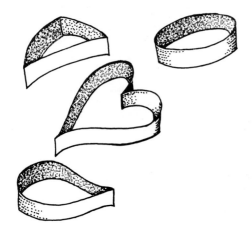

# ACTIVITY 11: SNOWFLAKE WALL HANGING

## Materials needed

White card; scraps of silver reflective paper or cooking foil; mother-of-pearl wrapping paper; thin white paper; white art straws; sugar lumps; sequins; silver glitter; silver or white paper doilies; white net or calico; dowelling; glue; twine or 2 cup hooks.

## What to do

To make the snowflakes, draw three times around an equilateral triangle placed on the folded edge of a piece of thin white paper. Cut out the whole shape, then fold it as shown. Cut patterns in the sides, through all the layers, to produce the snowflakes.

Open the shape very carefully and decorate it with glitter, sequins or shapes cut from wrapping paper.

To make the decorated squares, cut squares from white card approximately the same size as the opened snowflakes. Decorate with silver foil triangle shapes or shapes cut from wrapping paper. Alternatively, use art straws cut to size and placed in a star shape, radiating from a central point. Decorate the spaces in between the straws with glitter, sequins, sugar lumps, or shapes cut from silver or white doilies.

To make the wall hanging, staple or glue a length of calico or white net on to a piece of dowelling rod. Position the snowflakes and decorated squares alternately and in rows to cover the material. Tie a piece of strong twine to each end of the dowelling rod and hang it over a hook in the wall. Alternatively, screw two cup hooks into the wall and place the dowelling across them.

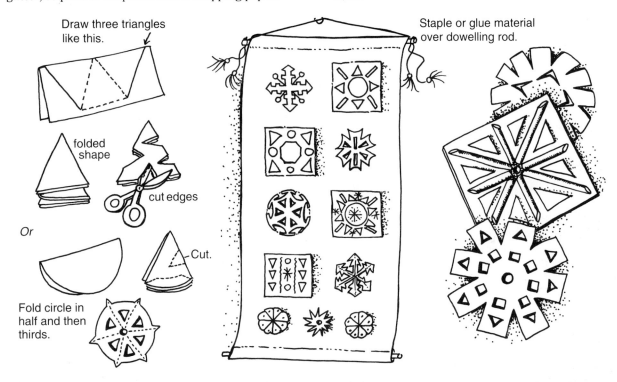

Draw three triangles like this.

folded shape

cut edges

Or

Fold circle in half and then thirds.

Cut.

Staple or glue material over dowelling rod.

# ACTIVITY 12: GLITTERED PINE CONES

## Materials needed

Pine cones; strips of felt or ribbon; double-sided foil; red or white paint; glitter; glue.

## What to do

Dip the pine cones in the red or white paint and leave to dry. Apply dabs of glue to the edges of the scales and sprinkle all over with glitter. Cut out three holly leaves from foil and glue these to the base of the pine cone. Then glue a loop of ribbon or felt to the bottom for hanging.

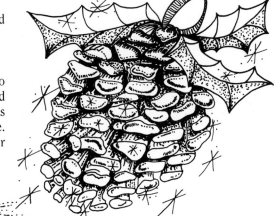

# ACTIVITY 13: CONE STARS ▶

**Materials needed**
White cartridge paper or double-sided coloured foil; glue or small stapler; crêpe paper or ribbon.

**What to do**
Star shapes can be made by placing a number of cones together. Each cone is made from a square of paper. Cut a square from white cartridge paper or double-sided foil. Draw two opposite corners towards each other, overlapping until they form a point at the base. Glue or staple together. Take care to obtain a good point. The children will need to have lots of practice in making these component cones.

A simple star shape uses twelve cones of the same size glued on to a base card. By using cones of different sizes the children will be able to create their own designs, but make sure they produce a balanced star with cones of equal size placed symmetrically. If the children work in groups, large-scale stars can be produced. The stars can be hung as mobiles, using strips of crêpe paper or ribbon.

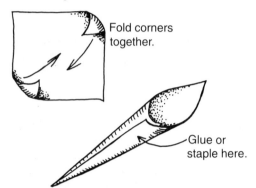

Fold corners together.

Glue or staple here.

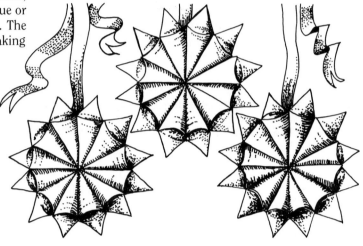

# ACTIVITY 14: ROCKING ROBIN ▶

**Materials needed**
Large paper plate; brown and yellow activity paper; brown and red crêpe paper or tissue; glue; gold foil; two adhesive black dots; masking tape; Blu-tack.

**What to do**
Using the blunt edge of a pair of scissors or a knitting needle, score across the centre of the front of the plate and fold it in half. This is the body of the robin. Cut out feather shapes from the brown crêpe paper or tissue and a smaller number from the red. (A template can be used for these if necessary.) Apply a little glue to the back of the open plate and, starting at the bottom, place the feathers in rows. Remind the children to overlap the feathers as they work along the rows and towards the top of the plate. As they near the top, they should change to red feathers to represent the robin's red breast.

For the robin's tail, cut a length of brown activity paper 14 cm long, and for the wings cut two wing shapes 10 cm long. Fold the plate in half again and glue the tail along the fold. Tuck the wings into the feathers on either side of the body and glue in place.

Next cut two circles of brown activity paper, 12 cm in diameter, for the head and two small circles of gold foil for the eyes. Stick a gold circle on each brown circle, then stick a small adhesive black dot in the centre of each gold circle for the pupil of the eye. Cut a diamond shape from yellow paper and fold it in half to make a beak.

Apply glue to the back of both head circles. Place one circle on one side of the body, then place the beak in position and the other head circle on the other side of the body, sandwiching the beak in between the two. This will need to be done carefully to ensure that the eyes are in the right position.

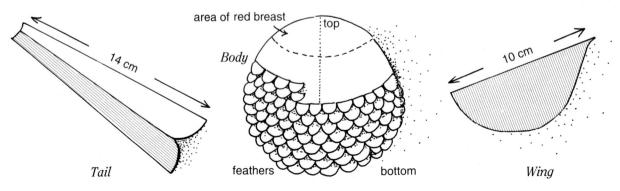

area of red breast

top

*Body*

14 cm

*Tail*          feathers          bottom          *Wing*

10 cm

44

A bridge of masking tape across the bottom of the body will help to keep the bird upright, and a piece of Blu-tack placed just under the head will help the rocking motion when the head is tapped gently.

A slightly simpler and less time-consuming version for younger children involves painting the paper plate brown, then cutting a semi-circle of red foil for either side to represent the red breast. The rest of the bird is made in the same way.

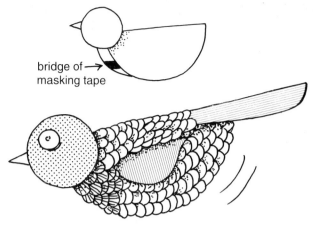

bridge of → masking tape

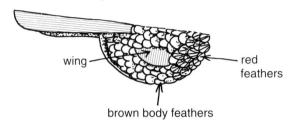

wing — red feathers

brown body feathers

# ACTIVITY 15: MINI CHRISTMAS GARLAND

## Materials needed
Card; pair of compasses; cotton wool; glue; green parcel ribbon; red sequins; red or tartan ribbon or velvet bow; metallic thread.

## What to do
Draw a circle 12 cm in diameter on the card. Cut it out, then in the centre of this circle draw another circle 5 cm in diameter and cut it out to create a cardboard ring.

Make a long sausage of cotton wool and glue it to one surface all the way round the ring.

Take a length of green parcel ribbon and sellotape one end to the back of the card ring. Wind it all the way round the ring, not too tightly, but making sure that the cotton wool is covered. Make a bow from red or tartan ribbon, or use a small ready-made bow, and glue it to the top of the garland. Stick red sequins on the garland and add a loop of metallic thread to hang it from the tree.

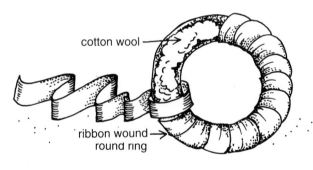

cotton wool

ribbon wound → round ring

# ACTIVITY 16: VICTORIAN GARLAND

## Materials needed
Green activity paper or tissue paper; glue.

## What to do
Cut out circles from the green paper, approximately 15 cm in diameter. The more circles you cut the longer the garland will be. Fold each circle into quarters and cut out a curved petal-shaped edge. Then make curved cuts down both sides, in alternate order, as shown.

Gently unfold the circles and glue them together in pairs, petal to petal, by spreading a little glue around the outside edges. Add a dab of glue in the centre of each circle on the opposite side to the glued outer edge.

Build up the garland by gluing the sets of circles together at the centre points. When dry, carefully pull apart to extend the garland and drape around the classroom.

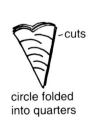

cuts

circle folded into quarters

edges of circle glued together

centres glued together

# ACTIVITY 17: GLITTER CORK

**Materials needed**
Cork; metallic thread; glitter; sequins; glue.

**What to do**
Tie a piece of metallic thread around the cork so that it can be hung. Older children, using a thimble, can push a darning needle through the centre and knot the end of the thread at the bottom. Cover the cork in glue and stick sequins all over it or roll it in glitter. Smartie tubes or other small containers treated in the same way look equally good if you want something larger.

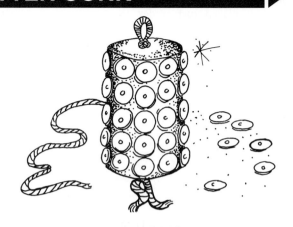

# ACTIVITY 18: SHINY SPIRALS

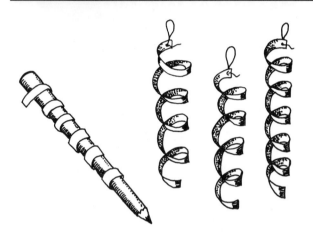

**Materials needed**
Double-sided foil craft paper; pencil, paintbrush or wooden spoon; metallic thread.

**What to do**
Cut out strips of foil, 2 cm × 30 cm. Wind each strip carefully around the pencil (or paintbrush or handle of the wooden spoon), then pull it out to leave the foil spiral. Make a hole in one end of the foil and loop a 10 cm piece of metallic thread through it to hang from the tree.

# ACTIVITY 19: PAPER STRAW STARS

**Materials needed**
Card; art straws; gold or silver spray paint; coloured foil; glitter; sequins; glue; thread or ribbon.

**What to do**
Cut a small circle of card. Cut the straws to half the length of the diameter of the star you wish to make. Flatten the straws and glue them in a radiating pattern from the centre of the circle of card. Make sure you space them out evenly for the best effect. Spray them with gold or silver spray paint: this should be done in a well-ventilated area.

Cut out a small foil star or a shape from a gold or silver doily and glue this in the centre of the card circle. Decorate the ends of the flattened straws with glitter and sequins. Attach a loop of thread or ribbon to the end of one of the straws and hang from the tree.

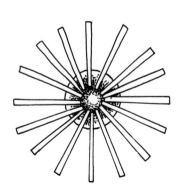

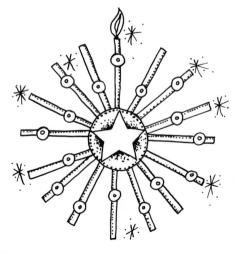

# ACTIVITY 20: EGG BOX BAUBLE

**Materials needed**

Egg carton; gold or silver spray paint or poster paint; sequins; glitter; braid; glue; ribbon or wool; crêpe paper or tissue paper.

**What to do**

Cut out two of the egg-holding sections from the egg carton. Make a hole in the centre of one section and pass a length of wool or ribbon through, knotting it on the inside. This is to enable the finished bauble to be hung. Glue the sections together and paint or spray them. When dry, decorate the outside with glitter, sequins or braid.

If you wish to have a hanging tassel, make a hole and insert a thread through the bottom section before gluing them together. To make the tassel, cut a fringe in a length of crêpe paper or tissue. Put a little glue on the end of the thread and apply glue along the top of the fringed strip. Roll up the strip into a tube around the thread and leave to dry. For extra decoration, put glass beads on the thread before adding the tassel.

You can make bigger baubles by using foil pastry cases. To create a string of baubles, thread them together one below the other to be hung as mobiles.

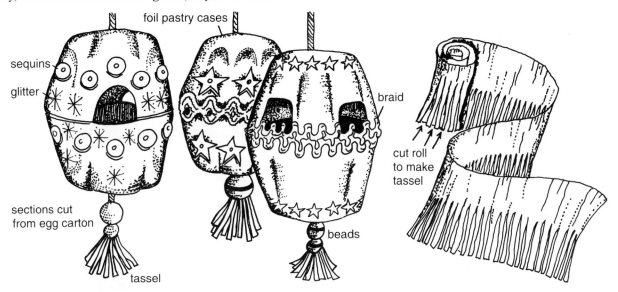

# ACTIVITY 21: FOIL STARS

**Materials needed**

Double-sided foil; parcel ribbon; petit four cases; gold or silver spray paint; scraps of tinsel or small baubles; gold or silver doilies; glue.

**What to do**

Cut out star shapes from the double-sided foil. In a well-ventilated place spray the petit four cases gold or silver. Cut out shapes from the doilies and stick one on the centre of each star, then stick a petit four case in a contrasting colour in the centre of that. Decorate the centre of the case by gluing into it a piece of tinsel or a small bauble.

To hang on the tree, make a small hole in the top of the star and tie a loop of thin parcel ribbon through it. The star can be decorated in the same way on the other side if you want a double-sided star, or two stars can be stuck back to back for extra strength.

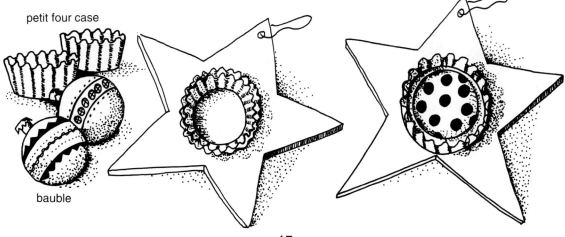

47

# ACTIVITY 22: PASTA BAUBLE

**Materials needed**
Card; coloured foil; pasta shapes; silver spray paint; glitter; sequins; PVA glue; ribbon.

**What to do**
Cut out a circle of card about 6 cm in diameter. Spread glue over the surface and make a pattern with pasta shapes. When set, spray with silver paint – do this in a well-ventilated place – and leave to dry. Cut out a star or bauble shape from the coloured foil and stick the decorated circle on to it. Brush the pasta shapes with a little PVA glue and sprinkle with glitter; you could also add a few sequins. Make two baubles of the same shape and stick them back to back with a loop of ribbon in between to enable the decoration to be hung.

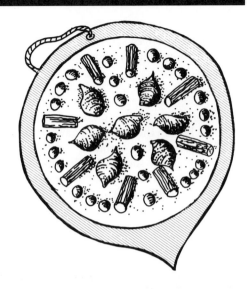

# ACTIVITY 23: TREE POM-POM

**Materials needed**
Balls or part balls of knitting wool; empty yoghurt or cream carton; 10p piece; card.

**What to do**
Draw two circles on the card, using the rim of the yoghurt carton to draw around. Then put the 10p piece in the middle of each circle in turn and draw around it. Cut out the two large circles, then cut out the smaller circles in the centre to create two card rings. Choose your wool (metallic wools look attractive) then, holding the two rings together, wind the wool all the way round until the ring is covered and the centre hole is filled in.

Cut from the outer edge to the centre of each card ring and remove carefully. Fluff up the pom-pom and hang from the tree. Small shiny sequins stuck on the ends of some of the strands will add a little sparkle.

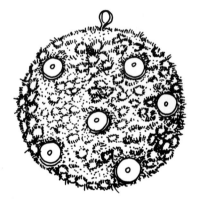

**To make a robin pom-pom**
Make a pom-pom as above, using brown wool for three-quarters of the circle and red wool for the rest. Cut a diamond-shaped piece of black felt, fold it in half and glue into place for the beak. Add felt eyes, tail and feet.

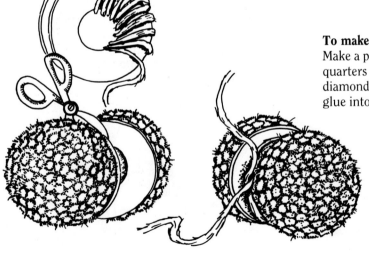

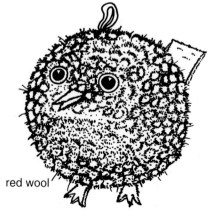

red wool

With scissors cut through all the thicknesses of wool at the outer edge. Cut off a 1 metre length of matching wool and wind it between the two card rings. Pull, then tie firmly, knotting the ends together to make a loop.

# ACTIVITY 24: SWEET CHAIN

**Materials needed**
Lots of wrapped sweets (those wrapped in coloured foil and cellophane with a twisted end are ideal); large needle; strong thread.

**What to do**
Make sure that the thread is long enough for your chain, then tie a knot at one end. Thread the needle and carefully push it through the twisted end of the wrapping paper round the sweets.

When all the sweets are threaded, knot the end of the thread and hang the garland on the tree. Join two or three of these together to make a really long garland that can be wound all around the tree.

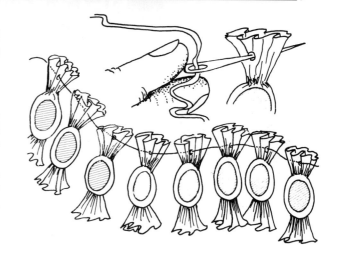

# ACTIVITY 25: MR SNOW

**Materials needed**
White, black and orange felt; thin card; firm black card; large white wooden bead; red ribbon; needle and thread; cotton wool; glue; a saucer.

**What to do**
Place the saucer on a piece of white felt and draw around it with a felt-tip pen. Cut out the circle. Sew around the edge of the circle, as shown, then pull the ends of the thread to draw the felt into a ball shape. Leave a gap in the top and the threads hanging. Draw a small circle, about 4.5 cm in diameter, on thin card, cut it out and push it into the bottom of the white felt ball. Fill the ball with cotton wool, pull the ends of the thread tightly and knot securely. Glue the wooden bead to the top of the ball to make the head. Cut a piece of ribbon to make a scarf and glue it in place around the neck. Use a black felt-tip pen to draw Mr Snow's face and stick on a piece of orange felt for his nose.

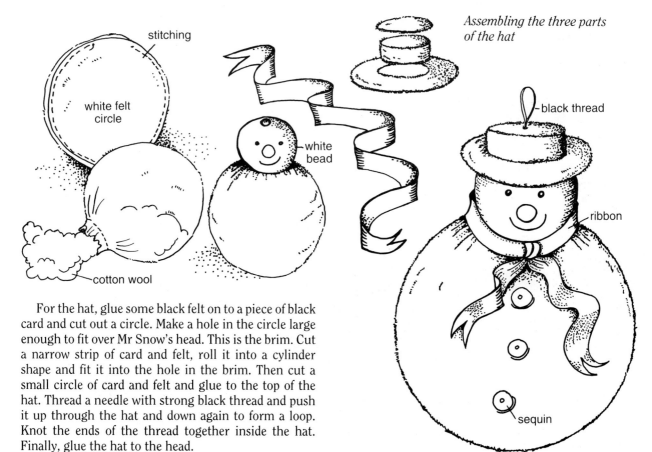

*Assembling the three parts of the hat*

stitching

white felt circle

cotton wool

white bead

black thread

ribbon

sequin

For the hat, glue some black felt on to a piece of black card and cut out a circle. Make a hole in the circle large enough to fit over Mr Snow's head. This is the brim. Cut a narrow strip of card and felt, roll it into a cylinder shape and fit it into the hole in the brim. Then cut a small circle of card and felt and glue to the top of the hat. Thread a needle with strong black thread and push it up through the hat and down again to form a loop. Knot the ends of the thread together inside the hat. Finally, glue the hat to the head.

49

# TABLE DECORATIONS

## ACTIVITY 1: FATHER CHRISTMAS CONE ▶

**Materials needed**
Red activity paper; cotton wool; white cartridge paper; pastels or chalks; glue.

**What to do**
Make a cone by cutting a semi-circle from the red activity paper. The radius of the semi-circle will be the height you wish your Father Christmas to be. Overlap the two corners of the semi-circle to make the cone and apply a little glue or sellotape them together.

Cut an oval shape from the white cartridge paper and draw eyes, nose and mouth on this with felt-tip pens. Glue the face on to the cone about half-way down. Make a moustache and a beard from cotton wool and glue in place. Trim the bottom of the cone with cotton wool also. Place a strip of cotton wool all round the cone just above the face to represent the fur trimming of the hat, then add a cotton wool ball to the point of the cone. Colour the cheeks and nose by rubbing in a little pink chalk or pastel.

## ACTIVITY 2: CONE CHRISTMAS TREE ▶

**Materials needed**
Green crêpe paper; card; coloured foil; sweets; glue.

**What to do**
Cut out a semi-circle from the card, with the radius equal to the height you wish your tree to be. Make a cone shape by curving over the two corners so that they overlap and secure them with glue or sellotape. Take a full roll of crêpe paper and cut a strip 4 cm wide from one end. Cut a fringe of 2 cm along one edge of the strip.

Start at the top of the cone shape and glue the end of the crêpe paper fringe to the point of the cone. Wrap the fringe around the cone in a spiral fashion, completely covering the card, until you reach the bottom. Decorate the tree with small circles cut from coloured foil and stick sweets on with double-sided tape. Cut out a foil star and glue to the top.

# ACTIVITY 3: CHRISTMAS CASTLE TABLE DECORATION

**Materials needed**
Card; small cardboard tubes of different lengths; white paint; black activity paper; blue foil; silver foil; cotton wool; large paper plate; glue.

**What to do**
Cover the back of the paper plate with silver foil; this will be the base. Make a cylinder from the card,

approximately 16 cm high and 7 cm in diameter for the main part of the castle. For the outer parts use two cardboard tubes of different lengths. Paint all the cylinders white and leave to dry. Next make three small cones to fit over the tubes. These will be the roofs of the towers so they should be slightly larger in diameter to overhang a little.

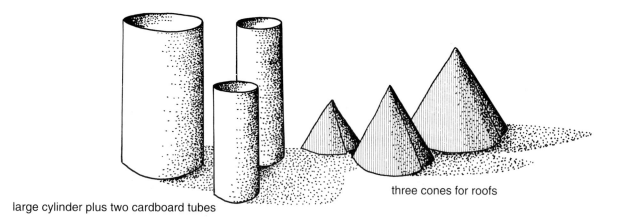

large cylinder plus two cardboard tubes

three cones for roofs

Glue the large cylinder to the middle of the base, then glue the other two cylinders on either side. Fix the cones to the top of the cylinders.

Cut out several arched window shapes from the blue foil and a doorway from the black activity paper. Stick these to the walls of the towers. Cut out a picture of

Father Christmas from an old Christmas card and glue it to the side of the doorway. Add a few sprigs of holly or other evergreens to the sides and back of the castle and place the whole thing on a bed of cotton wool. If you wish, it could be sprayed with a little artificial snow and sprinkled with glitter.

paper plate

# ACTIVITY 4: PLASTIC NETTING TREE

**Materials needed**
Length of plastic garden netting with mesh of 2 cm or finer; paper doilies or tissue paper; cooking foil or crêpe paper; waste-paper basket for the tub; twist ties; glue; coloured foil; tinsel.

**What to do**
Cover the waste-paper basket with cooking foil or crêpe paper. Shape the plastic netting into a cone and secure with twist ties. Take the paper doilies or cut large circles of tissue paper and scrunch them up in the middle to make pointed shapes. Insert the pointed ends through the mesh to leave the folded ends sticking out. Continue until you have covered the cone shape completely. If you push several tissue shapes through each section of mesh the tree will look better and the extra tissue will help to keep the individual shapes in place. When the tree is covered with tissue, glue it on to the foil-covered waste basket.

To decorate, cut out circles of coloured foil to stick on the ends of the tissue shapes and hang lengths of tinsel on the tree. Add a star at the top.

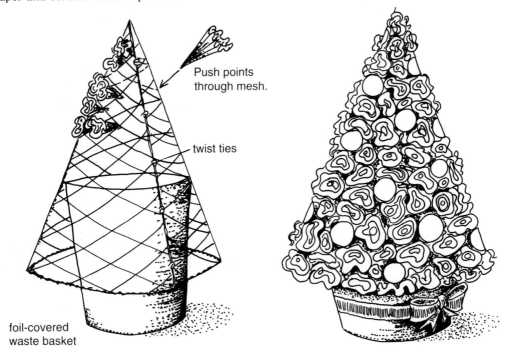

Push points through mesh.

twist ties

foil-covered waste basket

# ACTIVITY 5: SWEET TREE

**Materials needed**
Fallen branch from a tree; white emulsion paint or silver spray paint; silver glitter; PVA glue; large plant pot; sand.

**What to do**
Go to the nearest woodland or park or look around the school grounds to find a fallen branch of a suitable size (remind the children not to damage trees). Take the branch indoors and allow it to dry out, then either spray it with silver paint (in a well-ventilated area) or paint it with white emulsion paint. Leave it to dry thoroughly. Brush small areas of each branch with a little PVA glue and sprinkle glitter over it to give a frosty appearance. When this has dried, stand the branch in a large plant pot containing sand.

Decorate it with a Sweet Chain (see page 49) or make up small parcels of dolly mixtures or jelly babies, and add some brightly coloured lollipops. A healthier alternative might be to make up parcels of dried fruits and nuts to hang on the tree.

# ACTIVITY 6: FIR CONE CHRISTMAS TREE

**Materials needed**

Large fir cone; dark green paint or gold or silver spray paint; cotton reel or cardboard tube; parcel ribbon or braid; sequins; glitter; glue.

**What to do**

Use the largest fir cone you can find and make sure it is dry and fairly well open. Paint it with dark green paint or spray it with silver or gold paint (do this in a well-ventilated place). Leave the cone to dry, then glue it to one end of the cotton reel or a section of cardboard tube. Decorate the cone tree with sequins and glitter, and put a large sequin star at the top. You can thread lengths of thin parcel ribbon amid the 'branches' or push scraps of tinsel in between. Tie a length of wider parcel ribbon or braid around the cotton reel or cardboard tube.

If the cone is top heavy you can secure it with a little Blu-tack on the base of the cotton reel or glue it on to a paper plate covered with cotton wool to look like snow.

# ACTIVITY 7: YULE LOG

**Materials needed**

Split log; white soap powder; candle; holly, ivy or other available evergreens; unbreakable tree baubles; glitter; blunt knife or spatula; woodworking drill.

**What to do**

Drill a hole in the outside edge of the split log. The hole needs to be large enough for the candle. Mix the white soap powder with a little water until you have a thick paste. Use the blunt knife or spatula to spread the mixture on top of the log to look like snow. Place the candle in the hole and pile the paste around it to keep it secure.

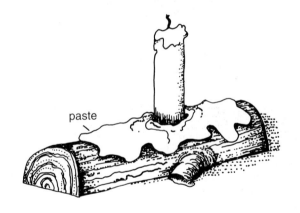

paste

Arrange the evergreens around the candle and along the top of the log place a few shiny baubles. Finally sprinkle the log with glitter to complete the effect.

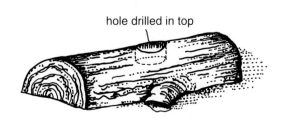

hole drilled in top

# ACTIVITY 8: CHRISTMAS ROSES

**Materials needed**

Red tissue paper; green pipe-cleaners; assorted evergreens, including holly, ivy, laurel and fir; small margarine tub; ready-mixed paint; PVA glue; plasticene; braid or ribbon.

**What to do**

Cut out eighteen squares of red tissue paper: six large ones (10 cm × 10 cm), six medium ones (8 cm × 8 cm) and six small ones (6 cm × 6 cm). Fold each square into four and draw a petal shape on the folded paper. Cut around the shape and unfold it carefully. Make three separate piles of large, medium and small flowers.

To make a rose, take one flower of each size. Put a small flower on top of a medium flower so that the petals are offset and use a spot of glue to hold them together. Place these on top of a large flower shape,

again with petals offset, and fix with a spot of glue. When you have made all six roses and the glue is dry, push a green pipe-cleaner through the centre of each flower and coil the end round. Gently curl and fold the petals into a rose-like shape.

Paint a small margarine tub with a mixture of two parts paint to one part PVA glue and decorate with braid or ribbon. Shape some plasticine into a large ball and place inside the tub, then push in the roses and arrange the greenery all around to hide the pipe-cleaner stems and the plasticene.

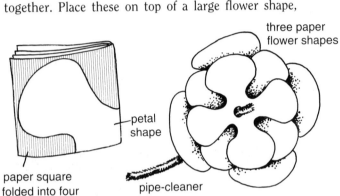

three paper
flower shapes

petal
shape

paper square
folded into four

pipe-cleaner

# ACTIVITY 9: CANDLE TABLE DECORATION

**Materials needed**

Round margarine tub; plasticene; cartridge paper; scrap of gold foil; red, orange and yellow tissue paper; florist's ribbon; shiny unbreakable baubles; evergreens; poster paint; PVA glue; glitter.

**What to do**

Mix the poster paint with the PVA glue (two parts paint to one part glue) and paint the outside of the margarine tub. Make a tight tube of cartridge paper for the candle and secure with glue. Cut flame shapes from the tissue paper: large flames from the yellow tissue, medium-size flames from the orange tissue and small flames from the red tissue. The smallest flame shape should be cut from gold foil. Glue the flames together, then fix to the top of the candle. Trickle glue down from the top of the candle shape and sprinkle glitter over the glue.

Make a ball of plasticene and push a hole in the centre to hold the candle. Press the plasticene on to the bottom of the margarine tub. Squeeze it around the candle to hold it firmly. Now take sprigs of evergreens and press them into the plasticene around the base of the candle so that they reach over the top of the tub. Make a bow of florist's ribbon and glue it to the candle, then place several shiny baubles at the base.

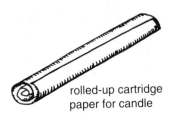

rolled-up cartridge
paper for candle

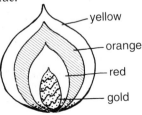

yellow

orange

red

gold

# ACTIVITY 10: CANDLE LIGHTS

**Materials needed**

Clear glass jamjars; enamel craft paints; nightlights (available in packs from hardware shops); paintbrushes; foil pastry cases.

**What to do**

Wash the jamjars very carefully, soak off the labels, rinse and dry. Dip a paintbrush in white enamel paint and cover the inside of the bottom of each jar to look like snow. On the outside of the jar you can paint a Christmas design, such as Father Christmas, a lantern or a Christmas tree. Let the paint dry, then decorate the jar all over with tiny spots of white to look like snowflakes.

When all the paint is dry put nightlights in foil pastry cases and place one in each jar. The nightlights should be lit with a long taper. Put the jars somewhere where they will not be knocked over. Remember never to touch the candle holders when they are lit or just after they have been blown out: they will be very hot.

An alternative way of decorating the jars is to cut shapes from coloured cellophane and glue them overlapping on to the outside of the glass.

painted designs

cellophane shapes

# ACTIVITY 11: GIANT CRACKER

**Materials needed**

Card; crêpe paper; glue; old Christmas card; sweets or small gifts; ribbon or braid.

**What to do**

Cut two strips of card 20 cm wide by 30 cm long. Cut one of the strips in half to make two strips 10 cm × 30 cm. Roll all three strips into cylinders of the same diameter and place them on a sheet of crêpe paper, 48 cm × 40 cm, as shown.

Glue the cylinders in place, then roll the card tubes in the crêpe paper to make one long cylinder. Glue the edge of the paper down to hold the cylinder shape. When the glue is dry, put some sweets or a small gift through one of the open ends into the centre of the cylinder. To make the cracker shape twist the two end rolls; this will also keep the gift in place. To decorate the cracker cut out a picture from an old Christmas card and glue it on to the central section of the cracker. The edges can be decorated with ribbon or braid.

crêpe paper

card cylinders

10 cm   20 cm   10 cm

40 cm

48 cm

# ACTIVITY 12: CHRISTMAS CRACKER PLACE MAT AND PLACE CARD

## Materials needed

*Place mat*
Rectangle of activity paper (30 cm × 20 cm); old Christmas card; coloured foil; gold or silver doily; glue; pinking shears.

*Place card*
Thin card (14 cm × 12 cm); sequins; braid.

## What to do

For the place mat, fold the rectangle of activity paper in half from the middle of the longer side. Make a triangular cut from the top and bottom edges, to a depth of 5 cm, through both layers. Cut triangles all the way down the open edges, again through both layers.

Open up the paper and you will have a cracker shape. Cut out a Christmas picture and glue it in the centre of a doily, then glue the doily in the centre of the cracker shape. Cut strips of coloured foil with pinking shears and decorate the cracker with them.

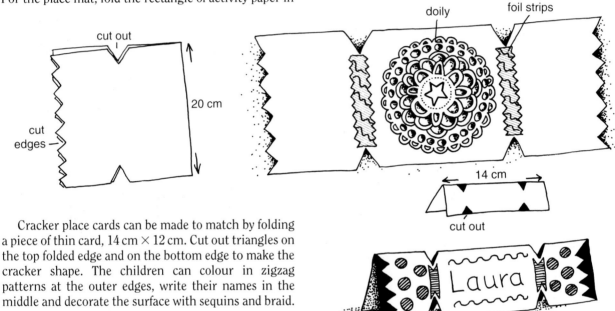

Cracker place cards can be made to match by folding a piece of thin card, 14 cm × 12 cm. Cut out triangles on the top folded edge and on the bottom edge to make the cracker shape. The children can colour in zigzag patterns at the outer edges, write their names in the middle and decorate the surface with sequins and braid.

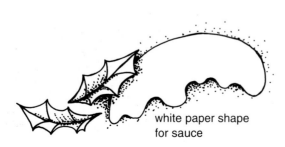

# ACTIVITY 13: CHRISTMAS PUDDING PLACE MAT

## Materials needed

White cartridge paper; black, red and brown wax crayons; green and red foil paper; glue.

## What to do

Draw a large pudding shape on a rectangle of white paper, 30 cm × 25 cm, covering as much of the paper as possible. Using a black wax crayon, draw on small black circles or dots to represent the currants in the pudding. Use a red crayon to draw red dots to represent cherries. Colour the rest of the shape with brown crayon for the pudding itself.

Cut out a semi-circle of white paper. Along the straight edge draw and cut out a wavy line to represent the white sauce. Glue this to the top of the pudding shape. Next cut some holly leaf shapes from green foil and some berry shapes from red foil. Glue these in place on top of the pudding. Finally, cut out the whole pudding shape from the rectangle and the place mat is complete. The wax crayon helps to make the mat more waterproof, which is helpful in case of spills.

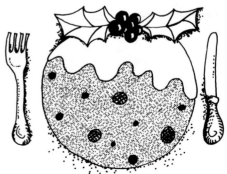

white paper shape for sauce

# ACTIVITY 14: CHRISTMAS PUDDING TABLE DECORATION

**Materials needed**

Brown paper bag (about 16 cm square); old newspapers; dark brown paint; black paint; sticky tape; white paper; glue; green and red foil paper; large paper plate.

**What to do**

Scrunch up some pieces of newspaper into a large ball and put them into the paper bag. Shape the bag into a pudding shape and fix the edges with sticky tape. Put the taped end at the bottom. Paint the paper-bag pudding dark brown, making sure you cover it well. When the paint is dry, use black paint to add lots of small black currants. On a sheet of white paper draw and cut out a wobbly starfish shape, about 12 cm across. Glue this to the top of the pudding to represent the white sauce trickling down the sides.

Cut out some holly leaves, about 5 cm long, from the green foil paper, put a spot of glue at one end and fix to the top of the pudding. Make some berries by cutting out 3 cm squares of red shiny foil. Roll the squares into balls between your fingers, put a spot of glue on each 'berry' and stick them between the holly leaves on the pudding. Glue the finished pudding on to a large paper plate, preferably one with a Christmas design around the edge.

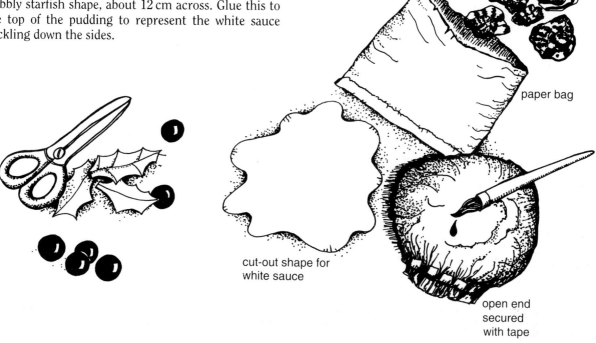

paper bag

cut-out shape for white sauce

open end secured with tape

paper plate

You can make smaller puddings in the same way to use as place cards. Use smaller paper bags and stick them on to small circles of card. Write the name on the card and decorate it.

*Smaller pudding place card*

Katie

# ACTIVITY 15: SWEET SURPRISE SNOWMAN ▶

**Materials needed**

Large plastic sweet jar; newspaper; cotton wool; glue; sticky tape; card; small piece of cardboard tube; sweets to fill the jar; coloured paper or felt; strip of material or crêpe paper.

**What to do**

Crumple a large sheet of newspaper into a ball and tape this firmly to the top of the lid of the jar to make the head. Tape crumpled newspaper to the sides of the jar to make a fat snowman shape. Cover the head and body with glue and stick cotton wool all over. Fill the jar with sweets.

Cut eyes, nose and mouth from coloured paper or felt and glue on to the snowman's face. Make a hat for the snowman by cutting a small piece of cardboard tube and two card circles, one the same diameter as the tube, the other slightly larger for the brim of the hat. Glue the pieces together and paint with black paint. Glue in place on the snowman's head. Make a scarf from a piece of scrap material or a strip of crêpe paper, place the snowman on a circle of cotton wool, surrounded by a few evergreens and shiny baubles.

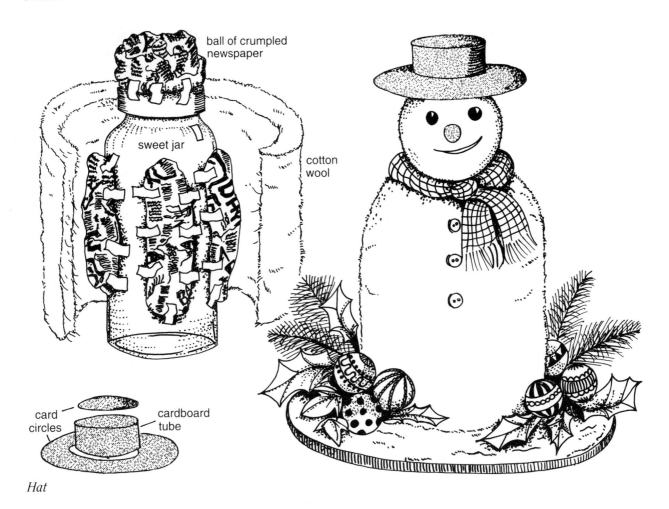

ball of crumpled newspaper

sweet jar

cotton wool

card circles

cardboard tube

*Hat*

# ACTIVITY 16: BALLOON FACES ▶

**Materials needed**

Lots of different-shaped balloons; thick felt-tip pens; glitter; sequins; cotton wool; coloured activity paper; Copydex adhesive; corrugated paper; strips of material and braid.

**What to do**

Blow up the balloons and draw faces on them with felt-

tip pens. Use Copydex to stick on sequins, cotton wool, material and paper shapes to decorate the faces.

Make tubes from pieces of corrugated paper and glue them to the balloons to make stands. The corrugated paper stands can be decorated to form part of the balloon face. Stick on strips of material and braid to represent the clothes the character is wearing. Stand the balloon faces in different places on the table.

*Clown*

*Lady*

*Snake*

# ACTIVITY 17: DECORATED COCKTAIL STICKS AND STRAWS

**Materials needed**
Old Christmas cards; cocktail sticks; bendy straws; Copydex adhesive.

**What to do**
Brighten up cocktail sticks by decorating them with small festive pictures cut from old Christmas cards. Dip one end of the cocktail stick into the Copydex adhesive and stick it on to the back of the picture. Leave to dry. Alternatively, use a small piece of sellotape. The sticks

can be used for cubes of cheese or pieces of fruit. Illustrations of festive food can be cut from magazines and stuck on to card to highlight different foods on the party table, if you wish.

Large cut-out pictures can be used for decorating straws. Cut slits at the top and bottom of the picture and carefully thread the straw through. Bend the top of the straw away from the back of the picture to make it easy to see what you are drinking!

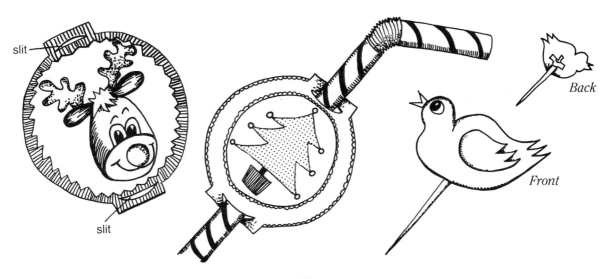

slit

slit

*Back*

*Front*

59

# ACTIVITY 18: ROBIN PLACE CARDS

**Materials needed**

Egg carton; white card; yellow card; paints; cotton wool; glue.

**What to do**

Cut out three sections from the egg carton and trim them evenly. Glue two sections together and paint the shape to look like a robin, with a brown body and a red breast. Cut out a tail and wings from card and paint them brown. Cut a diamond shape from yellow card and fold it in half for the beak. Glue these features in place to complete the robin.

Paint the third egg-carton section orange to look like a plant pot. Glue cotton wool around the base and then glue the robin on the top. Cut a rectangle of white card, write the name on it and glue it to the front of the plant pot.

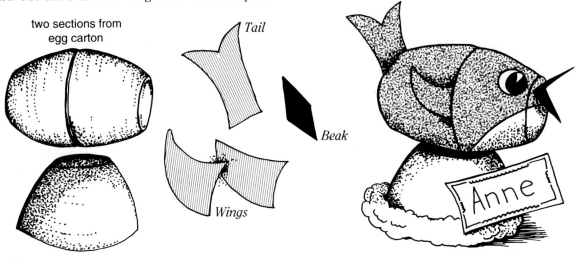

two sections from egg carton

*Tail*

*Beak*

*Wings*

Anne

# ACTIVITY 19: DOUGH CANDLE HOLDER

**Materials needed**

Salt dough (2 cups plain flour, 1 cup salt, 1 cup water); rolling pin; paint or felt-tip pens; polyurethane varnish; candles.

**What to do**

To make the salt dough, use a cup to measure the flour and salt into a bowl. Mix together then add water and stir with a fork until you have a firm dough. Knead the mixture until it is smooth: the dough should look like putty.

Pre-heat the oven to 160°C/325°F/gas mark 3. Roll out the pastry into a fat sausage and shape into a ring. Wet the edges to join them. Take a candle and make five evenly spaced holes in the ring by pressing the candle into the dough almost down to the base. You can make some holly leaves out of the dough, if you wish, and also little balls for the holly berries. Use a little water to stick them in the spaces between the holes. Put the decorated ring on a baking tray and cook for one hour. Leave to cool overnight, then next day paint and varnish it.

When completely dry, place candles in the holes and fill the space in the centre with evergreens and shiny baubles. Be very careful when the table decoration is lit and make sure you blow out the candles before they burn right down.

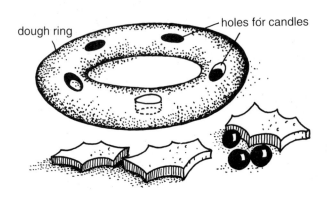

dough ring

holes for candles

60

# ACTIVITY 20: CHRISTMAS TREE TEA COSY

**Materials needed**

Card (30 cm × 70 cm); green felt; tinsel; sequins; scraps of coloured felt; Copydex adhesive; needle and thread; teapot.

**What to do**

Fold the card in half along the longer edge. Draw a large Christmas tree on the card, making sure that the point of the tree is in the centre of the top edge and the bottom of the tree extends right to the bottom edge of the card on both sides.

Cut out the Christmas tree shape from the folded card to give two trees of equal size. Spread the card shapes with Copydex and place on a large piece of green felt. Cut around the tree shapes, leaving a 1 cm border around each shape. When the glue is dry, curve the card shapes inwards and sew the edges of the felt together. Leave the middle section of the tree unsewn to allow for the handle and the spout of the teapot: test for fit on a standard-size teapot. Decorate the cosy with scraps of felt, tinsel and shiny foil to look like Christmas tree decorations. The card inside will help the tree to remain upright.

You can experiment with different shapes for tea cosies. Another suitably festive shape might be a Christmas pudding.

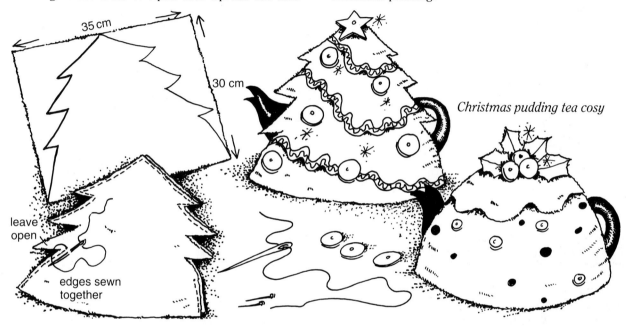

*Christmas pudding tea cosy*

# ACTIVITY 21: CHRISTMAS EGG COSIES

**Materials needed**

Card; pieces of coloured felt; assorted materials for decoration; glue or needle and thread.

**What to do**

Egg cosies are very easy to make from felt and can add a festive touch to the breakfast table on Christmas morning. Simply cut out two shapes in felt large enough to cover an egg. Use a card template to get two identical shapes. The felt shapes can be sewn or glued together and decorated as snowmen, Father Christmas, puddings or Christmas trees.

61

# CHRISTMAS COOKING

## ACTIVITY 1: YULE LOG

**Materials needed**
Blunt knife; plate; bowl.

**Ingredients**
Packet of round ginger biscuits; fruit juice; thick cream; cocoa; glacé cherries; angelica.

**What to do**
Put the biscuits in a bowl and soak them in fruit juice. Before they become too soggy to handle, stack them together on a plate to form a log shape. Pour extra juice over the biscuits then cover the top of the log with thick cream and sprinkle with cocoa. Put in the fridge to chill. Make sprigs of holly from cherries and angelica and use to decorate the log. You can add a robin cake decoration too, if you wish.

ginger biscuits

## ACTIVITY 2: ORANGE PUDDINGS

**Materials needed**
Small pudding basins; small plates; measuring jug; saucepan; spoon.

**Ingredients**
Packet of orange jelly; about 200 grams Christmas cake; the juice of an orange; thick cream; glacé cherries; angelica.

**What to do**
Make up the orange juice to 300 millilitres with water. With adult supervision the children can heat a little of the liquid to melt the jelly, then pour in the rest when the jelly is dissolved. Crumble the Christmas cake and stir into the jelly. Pour the mixture into small pudding basins and leave to set. Turn out the jellies on to small plates and pile whipped cream on top of each jelly. Decorate with glacé cherries and angelica.

# ACTIVITY 3: FIR CONE BISCUITS

**Materials needed**
Mixing bowl; wooden spoon; sieve.

**Ingredients**
Packet of round chocolate biscuits; large packet of chocolate buttons; 100 grams soft margarine; 100 grams icing sugar; 50 grams cocoa.

**What to do**
Put the margarine into the mixing bowl and add the icing sugar and cocoa through a sieve. Mix well together, then spread thinly over each biscuit. Press the chocolate buttons on to the mixture and overlap them to make the biscuits look like fir cones, then dust lightly with icing sugar.

# ACTIVITY 4: CHRISTMAS CANDLE CAKES

**Materials needed**
Knife; mixing bowl; spoon; small plates.

**Ingredients**
Chocolate Swiss roll; 6 chocolate flakes; 50 grams icing sugar; 1 teaspoon warm water; 3 glacé cherries.

**What to do**
Cut the Swiss roll into six thick slices and put on small plates. Push a chocolate flake into each slice so that it stands up. Make a paste by mixing icing sugar and water and put a blob of this on top of each flake. Stick half a glacé cherry in the middle of the paste to look like a candle flame.

# ACTIVITY 5: SUGAR SWEETS

**Materials needed**
Small bowl; large bowl; whisk; sieve.

**Ingredients**
225 grams icing sugar; 1 small egg white; flavouring (strawberry, banana or peppermint); colouring if desired (red for strawberry, green for peppermint); alternatively dip half of each sweet into melted chocolate.

**What to do**
Sieve the icing sugar into a large bowl. Whisk the egg white and add a few drops of flavouring, and colouring if desired. Add the egg white to the icing sugar and knead until the mixture is doughlike and stiff. Roll into small balls and flatten the tops then leave the sweets to harden. You could wrap them in small parcels to hang on the Christmas tree.

# ACTIVITY 6: COCONUT SNOWBALLS

**Materials needed**
Whisk; mixing bowl; sieve; small bowl; tray.

**Ingredients**
225 grams icing sugar; 1 egg white; peppermint flavouring; desiccated coconut.

**What to do**
Sieve the icing sugar into a bowl. Whisk the egg white, add a few drops of peppermint flavouring, then add to the icing sugar. Knead until the mixture is stiff and doughlike. Shape into small balls and then roll the balls in the desiccated coconut. Place on a tray and leave to harden.

# ACTIVITY 7: MARZIPAN SHAPES

**Materials needed**
Small biscuit cutters in various shapes; rolling pin; pastry board; baking tray lined with foil; oven gloves; palette knife; piping bag and nozzle.

**Ingredients**
Packet of marzipan; red and green natural food colouring; icing sugar; tiny edible silver balls; hundreds and thousands.

**What to do**
Pre-heat the oven to 180°C/350°F/gas mark 4. Divide the block of marzipan into three. Put one piece of marzipan on a worktop or board lightly sprinkled with icing sugar and knead until smooth. Put two or three drops of red food colouring on to the second piece of marzipan and knead to spread the colour evenly. Mix the green colouring into the third piece of marzipan in the same way.

Roll out each piece of marzipan on a board lightly dusted with icing sugar. The thinner you roll it out the more shapes you will be able to get from it, but do not make it too thin. Cut out shapes with the small biscuit cutters. An alternative is to make card templates in the shape of Christmas stockings, crackers and so on; these will be easy to draw and cut round. Using a palette knife, carefully lift the shapes on to the baking tray and cook for five minutes only. Wear oven gloves when taking them out of the oven. Leave to cool.

To decorate, draw simple designs using a piping nozzle on a tube of icing. Alternatively, put icing dots all over the shapes and press a silver ball into each one, or pipe icing in lines over the shapes then sprinkle on hundreds and thousands. If the shapes are stored in a dry place they will keep for about two weeks.

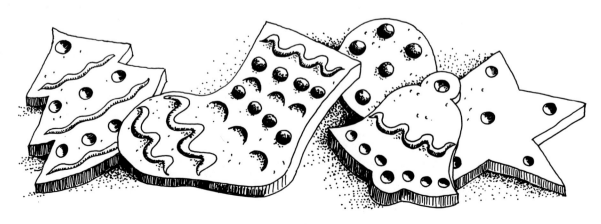

64

# ACTIVITY 8: CHRISTMAS LOGS

**Materials needed**
Knife; pyrex plate; whisk; pastry brush.

**Ingredients**
Packet of marzipan; 50 grams flaked almonds; beaten egg white.

**What to do**
Roll the marzipan into a long sausage shape about 3 cm in diameter, then cut into logs about 8 cm long. Spread the flaked almonds on a pyrex plate and place them under a hot grill for a few minutes until toasted. Chop them finely. Brush the logs with a little beaten egg white and roll them in the toasted almonds. Leave the ends of the logs uncovered. Allow the logs to dry for a few hours before eating.

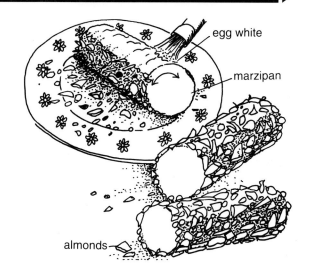
egg white
marzipan
almonds

# ACTIVITY 9: CORNET CLOWNS

**Materials needed**
Ice cream scoop; saucepan; pyrex bowl; large paper plate.

**Ingredients**
Ice cream; cornets; Smarties; angelica; chocolate chips; crystallised orange and lemon segments.

**What to do**
Melt some of the chocolate chips in a bowl over a saucepan of water. Decorate the cornets by sticking on Smarties with the melted chocolate. Arrange scoops of ice cream on the paper plate and put a cornet as a hat on each one.

Make the faces using chocolate chips, Smarties, angelica or orange and lemon segments. You will need to work quickly so that the ice cream does not melt. When finished store in a freezer until needed.

# ACTIVITY 10: SUGAR MICE

**Materials needed**
Whisk; mixing bowl; piping bag with nozzle; baking tray lined with parchment paper; blunt knife; cocktail stick.

**Ingredients**
125 grams caster sugar; 2 egg whites; 24 split almonds; 36 silver balls; red liquorice laces cut into 10 cm lengths.

**What to do**
Whisk the egg whites until they are frothy and stiff, then gradually whisk in the sugar. Put the mixture into a piping bag with a wide nozzle and pipe it evenly and thickly over a baking tray lined with parchment paper. Use a blunt wet knife to shape the mice, pushing the mixture into a rounded shape for the body and tapering down to a point for the head. Place split almonds above the pointed face shape to make ears and use silver balls for the eyes and nose. Bake in a very cool oven (110°C/225°F/gas mark $\frac{1}{4}$) for two hours. Allow the cooked mice to cool on the parchment, then use a cocktail stick to make a small hole in the tail end of each mouse. Stick a piece of liquorice in the hole to form the tail.

# ACTIVITY 11: COCONUT SNOWMEN

**Materials needed**
Mixing bowl; wooden spoon; tray lined with greaseproof paper; 10 cocktail sticks.

**Ingredients**
100 grams white breadcrumbs; 100 grams chopped nuts; 250 grams cream cheese; currants; slivers of carrot; slices of cucumber; thick slices of carrot; desiccated coconut.

**What to do**
Mix together the breadcrumbs, nuts and cream cheese in a mixing bowl. Divide the mixture into ten medium-size balls and ten small balls. Roll the balls in the desiccated coconut. Next take a slice of carrot and place it on top of a slice of cucumber. Push a cocktail stick down through both slices and then into one of the small balls so that it goes right through: this makes the hat and the head. Push the lower end of the cocktail stick into one of the large balls to attach the head to the body.

Make a nose for each snowman from a sliver of carrot and press in currants for the eyes, mouth and buttons. Place each finished snowman on a lined tray and store in a cool place until needed.

carrot
cucumber
cocktail stick

cocktail stick holding head on to body

# ACTIVITY 12: FATHER CHRISTMAS BISCUITS

**Materials needed**
2 mixing bowls; piping bag with medium nozzle; tray; blunt knife.

**Ingredients**
Packet of plain digestive biscuits; 100 grams icing sugar; natural red food colouring; marzipan; currants.

**What to do**
To make the icing, add 1 tablespoon of warm water to the icing sugar. Mix until smooth and divide into two. Add red food colouring to one bowl of icing and spread a little over the top part of each biscuit for the hat. Pour the white icing into the piping bag and pipe on the beard and moustache and furry rim for the hat. Use currants for the eyes and nose, stuck on with a little white icing, and add a marzipan mouth in the same way.

red icing
white icing
white icing

66

# ACTIVITY 13: VICTORIAN ORANGES AND LEMONS

**Materials needed**
Saucepan; pastry brush; two small bowls; large mixing bowl; large plate.

**Ingredients**

*For the oranges and lemons*
285 grams Carolina Rice (or cooked short-grain rice); 30 grams arrowroot; the rind of a lemon cut thinly; 115 grams sugar; $2\frac{1}{2}$ pints milk; 10 drops vanilla essence.

*For the syrup*
455 grams sugar; juice of three oranges; 15 grams gelatine dissolved in half a pint of water; pinch of saffron; egg yolk; lemon juice.

**What to do**
To make the oranges and lemons, mix all the ingredients together and boil until firm. Spread the mixture out on a plate, and when the dough is nearly cold, with floured hands mould the dough into orange and lemon shapes.

To make the syrup, heat the mixture of sugar, orange juice, and gelatine and water. While the syrup is still hot divide it into two bowls and add a pinch of saffron to one.

Finish off the oranges by brushing them with the saffron syrup. To finish off the lemons, coat them with a mixture of egg yolk and lemon juice and when they are dry brush them with some of the syrup without saffron.

In Victorian times these oranges and lemons were served with thick custard and chocolate biscuits.

# ACTIVITY 14: SWEET CHRISTMAS PUDDINGS

**Materials needed**
Large mixing bowl; wooden spoon; small dish; spoon; plate.

**Ingredients**
50 grams butter; 125 grams icing sugar; 2 tablespoons cocoa; 2 tablespoons double cream; a few drops of vanilla essence; 250 grams cake crumbs; chocolate sugar strands; 50 grams icing sugar; miniature plastic holly sprigs.

**What to do**
Cream the butter and icing sugar together and gradually add the cocoa, cream, vanilla essence and cake crumbs to the mixture. Roll the mixture into sixteen small balls, then roll the balls in the chocolate sugar strands. Mix 50 grams of icing sugar with a teaspoon of

hot water and place a small drop of icing on the top of each ball. Press a plastic holly sprig into the top of each pudding to complete it.

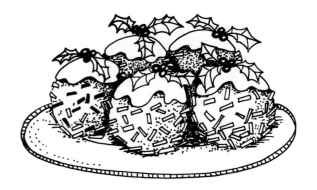

# ACTIVITY 15: MARSHMALLOW MINCE PIES

**Materials needed**

Circular pastry cutter; rolling pin; wire rack; patty tin.

**Ingredients**

125 grams ready-made shortcrust pastry; mincemeat; 12 pink and white marshmallows; 3 glacé cherries cut into quarters.

**What to do**

Roll out the pastry on a floured surface. With the pastry cutters cut out twelve circles and use these to line the patty tin. Spoon a little mincemeat into each pastry case and bake in a pre-heated oven, 200°C/400°F/gas mark 6, for ten to fifteen minutes. When the tarts are ready, remove them from the oven and place a marshmallow in the centre of each one. Return them to the oven just long enough to melt the marshmallows slightly. Remove from the oven, carefully place a piece of cherry on top of each tart and leave them to cool on a wire rack.

# ACTIVITY 16: PLUM PUDDING

**Materials needed**

Large bowl; wooden spoon; pudding dish; square of white cloth to wrap the pudding in; saucepan.

**Ingredients**

675 grams raisins; 225 grams currants; 335 grams breadcrumbs; 225 grams flour; 335 grams finely chopped beef suet; 9 eggs, well beaten; 1 wineglass of brandy; 225 grams chopped, mixed peel; half teaspoon grated nutmeg; pinch ground ginger.

**What to do**

Mix together the raisins, currants, breadcrumbs, flour, suet, mixed peel, grated nutmeg and ginger. Stir in the eggs and the brandy and mix thoroughly together. Put the white cloth into the pudding dish and spoon in the mixture. Tie the cloth by the corners to make a neat bundle, then steam for six hours over a saucepan of boiling water.

# ACTIVITY 17: CHOCOLATE DIP BISCUITS

### Materials needed
Mixing bowl; saucepan; baking trays; fork; small bowl.

### Ingredients
175 grams plain flour; 50 grams caster sugar; 100 grams margarine; 100 grams chocolate; a few drops vanilla essence.

### What to do
Rub the margarine into the flour. Add the vanilla essence and the sugar and knead the mixture into a firm ball. Divide into twelve small balls. Put them on a greased baking tray and press gently with a fork to flatten them. Bake at 190°C/375°F/gas mark 5 for 20 minutes. When the biscuits are cool, melt the chocolate in a bowl over hot water. Very carefully dip the biscuits in the chocolate and leave them to dry.

Dip into chocolate.

Press with a fork.

# ACTIVITY 18: CHEESY BISCUITS

### Materials needed
Mixing bowl; spoons; rolling pins; biscuit cutters in various shapes; baking trays.

### Ingredients
125 grams plain flour; $\frac{1}{4}$ teaspoon salt; 75 grams grated cheese; 75 grams margarine; 1 egg.

### What to do
Rub the margarine into the flour and salt, then add the grated cheese. Mix to a stiff paste with the egg, adding water if necessary. Roll out the mixture thinly and cut into shapes with the biscuit cutters. Bake on a greased baking tray at 180°C/350°F/gas mark 4 until slightly coloured and firm.

# ACTIVITY 19: PEPPARKAKOR BISCUITS

**Materials needed**

Sieve; 2 bowls; wooden spoon; foil; pastry board; rolling pin; pastry cutters; baking sheet; piping bag with nozzle.

**Ingredients**

400 grams flour; 1 teaspoon bicarbonate of soda; $1\frac{1}{2}$ teaspoons mixed ground ginger, cloves and cinnamon; 230 grams butter or margarine; 230 grams dark brown sugar; 2 egg whites.

*For icing*

250 grams icing sugar; 1 egg white; candied fruit or silver balls for decoration

**What to do**

Sift the flour, spices and bicarbonate of soda together. Mix the butter and sugar into a paste and beat in the egg whites. Slowly add the dry ingredients and mix them all together. Wrap the mixture in foil and store in a cold place for about twelve hours.

Heat the oven to 180°C/350°F/gas mark 4. Roll out the dough to about half a centimetre thick on a lightly floured board. Use the pastry cutters to cut out shapes and place the biscuits on an ungreased baking sheet, leaving a space between each one. Place them in the oven to cook for ten minutes or until light brown around the edges. Take the biscuits out and while they are cooling, prepare the icing. Make it stiff enough to pipe patterns on the biscuits. Decorate with silver balls or candied fruit.

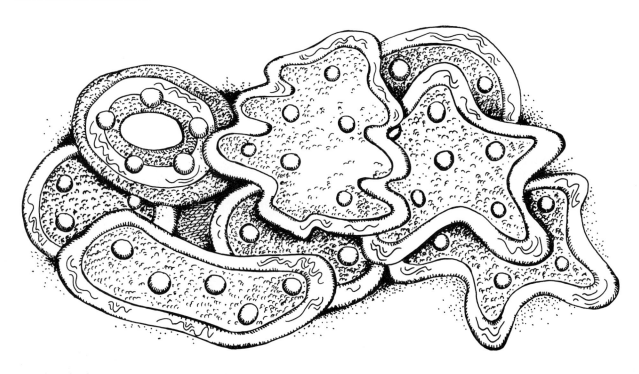

# ACTIVITY 20: COCONUT SQUARES

**Materials needed**

Mixing bowl; spoon; spatula; 2 small bowls; small rectangular baking tin.

**Ingredients**

450 grams icing sugar; 225 grams desiccated coconut; 6 tablespoons condensed milk; pink food colouring.

**What to do**

Mix the sugar and coconut with the condensed milk. Divide the mixture into two bowls. Add a few drops of food colouring to one bowl. Dust the baking tin with icing sugar and press in the mixture, one colour at each end. Mark into squares and leave to set.

# ACTIVITY 21: CHOCOLATE MEDALS

**Materials needed**

Mixing bowl; small saucepan; plate; wooden spoon; paper cake cases; sticky tape; coloured ribbons; coloured foil.

**Ingredients**

Large bars of chocolate.

**What to do**

This activity will need careful supervision as boiling water is involved. Break up the chocolate into a bowl. Heat some water in a saucepan until it is just beginning to boil. Stand the bowl over the saucepan on low heat and when the chocolate begins to melt, stir it until smooth. Place the cake cases on a plate and pour a little of the melted chocolate into each one. Put them in the fridge until they set hard.

Remove the chocolate discs from the paper cases and wrap each one in coloured foil. Secure the foil at the back with sticky tape. Now take a length of ribbon about 70 cm long for each medal and tape the ends to the back of the foil disc to make a loop that can be worn around the neck.

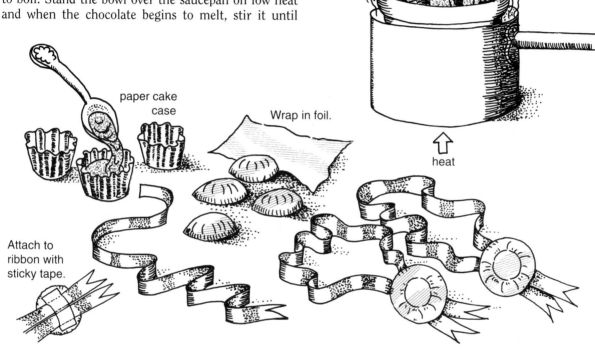

paper cake case

Wrap in foil.

heat

Attach to ribbon with sticky tape.

# ACTIVITY 22: BUTTERSCOTCH FUDGE

**Materials needed**

Heavy-bottomed saucepan; wooden spoon; whisk; buttered tray.

**Ingredients**

1 cup sweetened condensed milk; 2 cups caster sugar; 4 tablespoons butter; a few drops butterscotch essence; 4 tablespoons water.

**What to do**

Put the butter in the saucepan, followed by all the other ingredients. Warm over a low heat, stirring continuously, until the sugar has dissolved. The next stage should be carried out by an adult. Bring the mixture to the boil and continue boiling for ten minutes. Remove the pan from the heat and beat the mixture hard until it has thickened. This is very important or the fudge will not set.

Turn the mixture into a buttered tray and leave it in the refrigerator or a cool place until it is set. When it is ready the children can cut it into evenly sized squares. The fudge can be packed into a presentation box to be given as a present.

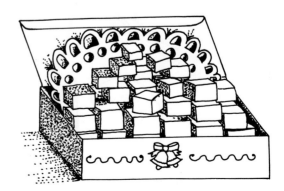

# ACTIVITY 23: HOLLY LEAF BISCUITS

**Materials needed**
Sieve; large basin; polythene bag; rolling pin; greased baking tray; round-ended knife or pastry cutter; mixing bowl; pastry board.

**Ingredients**
225 grams self-raising flour; $1\frac{1}{2}$ level teaspoons cinnamon; pinch of salt; 150 grams butter; 100 grams caster sugar; 1 egg.

*For the icing*
225 grams icing sugar; a few drops of green food colouring.

*For the berries*
Marzipan; a few drops of red food colouring.

**What to do**
Sift the flour, salt and cinnamon together in a basin, then rub in the butter until the mixture looks like breadcrumbs. Mix in the sugar. Beat the egg and add it to the mixture to make a stiff dough. Knead the dough, then put it into a polythene bag and leave it in the fridge for half an hour.

Roll out the dough to a thickness of 1 cm and cut into holly leaf shapes using a round-ended knife or a pastry cutter. Place the biscuits on a greased baking tray and bake for twelve to fifteen minutes at 180°C/350°F/gas mark 4. Leave the biscuits to cool and make the icing. Mix the icing sugar with enough water to make a fairly stiff paste. Colour it with green food colouring and spread on the biscuits when they have cooled. Add the red food colouring to the marzipan and roll it into small balls to make the berries. Press them into the moist icing and sprinkle with a little more icing sugar to give the appearance of snow.

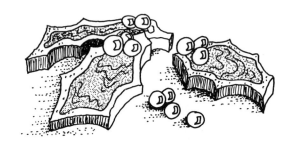

# ACTIVITY 24: ST NICHOLAS' LETTER BISCUITS

**Materials needed**
Greased baking sheet; rolling pin; round-ended knife; pastry brush; pastry board.

**Ingredients**
400 grams short-crust pastry; 200 grams marzipan; small quantities of flour, sugar and milk.

**What to do**
Set the oven to 220°C/425°F/gas mark 7. Sprinkle the board with flour to stop the pastry from sticking. Roll the pastry out thinly and cut into strips about 10 cm × 2 cm. Roll the marzipan into thin sausages about 10 cm long and sprinkle with a little sugar. Wrap

a strip of pastry around each piece of marzipan and dab a little milk along the edges, then gently press the two edges together.

Now bend each roll into the shape of a letter, taking care not to break it. Some letters can be made from one piece of pastry by bending and shaping; others will need to be made up from strips of different lengths. This can be done by sticking pieces of pastry together using the milk as a glue. Place the finished letters carefully on a greased baking sheet, leaving a little space between each one. Bake in the centre of the oven for ten to fifteen minutes. When the biscuits are golden brown, take them out and remove from the tray.

# ACTIVITY 25: CHOCOLATE APPLES

**Materials needed**
Saucepan half filled with boiling water; heatproof basin; wooden spoon; waxed paper; absorbent paper.

**Ingredients**
Eating apples; lollipop sticks; unsweetened cooking chocolate; chocolate vermicelli or hundreds and thousands.

**What to do**
Wash the apples and dry thoroughly on a sheet of absorbent paper. Push a lollipop stick firmly into each apple at the point where the stalk joins. Break the chocolate into small pieces and put into the heatproof basin. Place this on a pan of gently simmering water, remembering safety precautions.

When the chocolate is soft and runny, remove the basin from the saucepan and dip each apple in the chocolate. Make sure the apple is well covered by turning it round in the chocolate. Lift the apple out carefully and roll it in the vermicelli or the hundreds and thousands. Stand the apples, with the sticks pointing upwards, on the waxed paper and leave them in a cold place or the refrigerator to set.

**Chocolate cherries** can be prepared in the same way using glacé cherries and cocktail sticks.

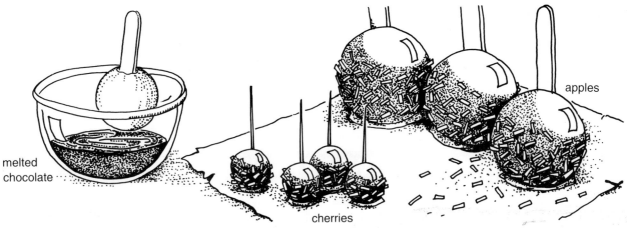

melted chocolate

apples

cherries

# ACTIVITY 26: BLACK BUN

This cake is traditionally eaten on New Year's Eve in Scotland and it should be made several weeks before New Year.

**Materials needed**
Mixing bowl; rolling pin; wooden spoon; 20 cm round cake tin; whisk; skewer; pastry brush.

**Ingredients**

*For the pastry*
200 grams plain flour; pinch of salt; 100 grams butter; egg yolk to glaze.

*For the filling*
400 grams currants; 400 grams raisins; 50 grams candied peel; 100 grams chopped blanched almonds; 100 grams plain flour; 100 grams soft brown sugar; 1 teaspoon each ground cinnamon, ginger, allspice, nutmeg; 1 level teaspoon cream of tartar; 1 level teaspoon bicarbonate of soda; 1 whisked egg; 2 tablespoons whisky; 3 level tablespoons black treacle.

**What to do**
Mix the ingredients for the pastry, add a little water to make a firm dough and knead. Mix all the filling ingredients together in a large mixing bowl. The treacle will need to be heated in a pan to make it soft and runny before adding it. Roll out two-thirds of the pastry and use it to line the greased cake tin, making sure that the pastry comes up above the sides of the tin. Spoon the filling into the pastry base. Roll out the remaining pastry to make a top for the tin. Moisten the edges of the pastry before you put the top on, then press the edges firmly together.

Use any left-over bits of pastry to make the letters for 'Happy New Year' and arrange on top. Then with a skewer make five or six holes in the top and press right down to the bottom of the cake. Glaze the top of the cake with egg yolk. The cake should be baked in the centre of the oven at 180°C/350°F/gas mark 4 for two-and-a-half hours. If the pastry seems to be getting too brown you can cover it with baking foil. Take the cake out of the oven and turn it out of the tin and allow to cool. It should be wrapped in foil and stored in an airtight container until ready to be eaten.

# ACTIVITY 27: NEW YEAR PUNCH

**Materials needed**
Saucepan; knife; glasses; paintbrush.

**Ingredients**
5 cloves; 1 orange; 2 bottles ginger beer; piece of cinnamon stick; caster sugar; beaten egg white.

**What to do**
Press the cloves into the orange and bake it in the oven for half-an-hour at 180°C/350°F/gas mark 4. Cool a little then slice the orange and put the pieces in a saucepan with the ginger beer and a piece of cinnamon stick. Heat the liquid gently, taking care not to let it boil. When the punch has cooled slightly serve it in frosted glasses.

*To frost the glasses*
With a fine brush, use the beaten egg white to paint the outside of the glasses with seasonal pictures, such as snowmen or winter trees. Put some caster sugar on a tray and roll the glasses in the sugar. This will stick to the egg white and the pictures will be shown clearly. Dip the rim of each glass in egg white and then in caster sugar. Leave the glasses to dry for a few hours before filling them with the special punch.

# ACTIVITY 28: TWELFTH NIGHT CAKE

This special cake was traditionally eaten on twelfth night. Sometimes a dried pea and a dried bean were put into the cake mixture, as in a Christmas pudding. The person finding the bean would become king and the person finding the pea would be queen.

**Materials needed**
Mixing bowl; wooden spoon; medium-size cake tin; greaseproof paper.

**Ingredients**
400 grams flour; 15 grams baking powder; pinch of salt; 1 teaspoon grated nutmeg; 225 grams butter; 225 grams caster sugar; 4 eggs; 400 grams currants; 115 grams mixed peel; 55 grams chopped almonds; 6 tablespoons brandy; 1 dried bean and 1 dried pea.

**What to do**
Cream the butter and sugar together and gradually beat in the eggs. Mix the flour, baking powder, salt and nutmeg and add to the butter mixture, followed by the rest of the ingredients. If you are using a bean and a pea, add them to the mixture. Grease and line a cake tin, pour in the mixture and bake in a pre-heated oven at 140°C/275°F/gas mark 3 for about three hours. At the end of this time leave the cake in the oven for thirty minutes with the heat off. Remove the cake from the tin and allow it to cool.

The cake can be iced and decorated if required.

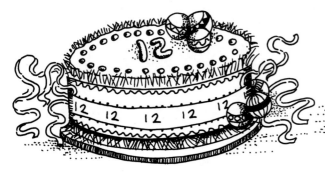

# SCENERY

The activities in this section are all intended as backdrops for a stage or performance area and involve a variety of materials, levels of constructional skill and time. They are all designed to be 2 metres high, since it is anticipated that this height will provide an attractive backdrop to performers on raised platforms and at the same time will provide higher visual interest when action takes place at a lower level.

The materials needed for the backdrops vary in cost. The most expensive items are commercially produced 2 metre deep rolls of corrugated card. This comes in lengths of about 30 metres and varies in price depending on the educational supplier. However, a resource of this kind can be recycled if only one side is used at a time or if the items made from it are stored for future performances, thus increasing its cost effectiveness. The card can be rolled up for easy storage. The width of the backdrop can be matched to the space available, but in most places a width of 2–3 metres is adequate and in terms of corrugated card the cost should be reasonable.

Curtains and lengths of cane and narrow wood are also suggested and items like these can often be obtained from parents or other community sources.

Good art papers, ready-mixed paint in bright colours, emulsion paint and sparkling seasonal papers are amongst the basic materials required. Throughout the section, large sizes, startling colours and colour contrasts are all indicated to make the most impact, since bright lighting and the distance of the audience tend to diminish the effect of all but the very obvious.

Whenever painting of a scene is indicated, we suggest you experiment with large implements such as paint rollers, emulsion brushes and sponges. With these you can make dabbed marks, streaks, twists and a variety of other patterns to produce a texture which need not necessarily give full cover but just an impression. This style of painting will use less paint, will weigh less on the background and will, of course, cost less.

Finally, the themes chosen for the backdrops are either related to the Christmas story or of a general festive style that will allow scope for individual needs.

# ACTIVITY 1: CHRISTMAS STAR ▶

## Materials needed

Curtain rail and fittings or wall stapler and wood; red, green and silver foil paper; silver plastic foil; white crêpe paper; large dark self-coloured curtain, about 2 m in depth.

## What to do

If a curtain rail can be fixed to the back wall of the most commonly used performance site this is very useful for hanging a variety of curtains and backdrops. However, if standard items like PE equipment prove an obstacle to this, have a strip or more of wood fixed to the wall and staple the curtain to this, taking it over the equipment which is in the way.

Gather the curtain with its strings or with the stapler as you fix it to the wall and let it drape in folds to the floor.

To decorate the edges and top, you will need to cut out from green foil paper as many 50 cm long holly leaves as you think you will need to fill the length. Cut out red berries about 15 cm in diameter, strips of white crêpe and silver plastic foil about 10 cm wide to hang almost to the floor, and a silver star about 50 cm across. Staple the decorations as shown to the top of the curtain.

2 m

red foil paper

green foil paper

strips of plastic foil or crêpe

PE equipment

staple    staple

floor    dark curtain

# ACTIVITY 2: BETHLEHEM ▶

## Materials needed

Large white bed sheet; emulsion paint or ready-mixed paints (sandstone, green, brown, dark blue, black); sponges, large brushes or rollers; lengths of wood (approx. 5 cm × 2.5 cm); 2 nails (8 cm approx.); 2 heavy metal hooks; rawl plugs; drill; wall stapler.

## What to do

This scene is painted freehand on to a sheet, which is then fixed to a hanger. It can either be assembled first and then painted in the position in which it will hang or the sheet can be stapled to a display board and painted. You will, however, need to staple a good pad of newspaper all over the board under the sheet to prevent the paint soaking through. This type of scenery is very durable and will last for many performances if stored rolled, with newspaper in between.

The hooks are fixed to the wall, with rawl plugs if necessary, and the wood hung as shown, with the sheet folded over the top and stapled into the wood. A similar piece of wood is fixed to the bottom in the same way to weigh down the sheet and keep it straight.

Paint goes on to fabric quite easily and you can use sponges, large decorating brushes or rollers to apply it. You do not need a solid matt coverage of paint to achieve the effect: often an outline and a touch of colour will suffice. Simple geometric building shapes with window and door shadows picked out in black should be easy to produce and effective. You can add items of free-standing scenery in front of the backdrop and staple self-coloured curtains to each side to hide the edges.

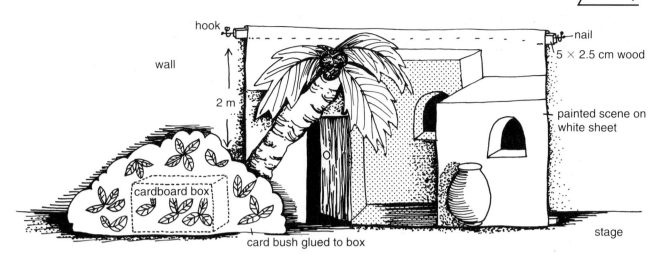

## ACTIVITY 3: STARDROP

**Materials needed**

Silver plastic foil and white crêpe paper (both cut to 2 m × 10 cm strips); silver foil paper; wall stapler; strips of wood as necessary.

**What to do**

Using a strip of wood, if necessary, as described in Activity 1, staple the strips of silver and white paper alternately across the width of the backdrop, gathering each strip a little and putting them close together to give fullness.

To finish off the top, cut out star shapes from the silver foil and glue or staple them across the ends of the strips.

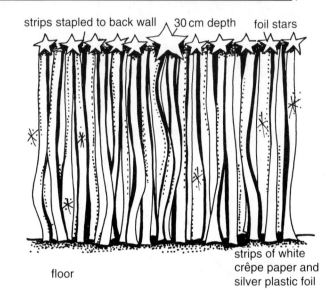

## ACTIVITY 4: STARSHINE

**Materials needed**

Cellophane in different colours (full roll width in 2 m drops or short rolls sellotaped together); assorted colours of foil paper stars (each about 40 cm depth); wall stapler.

**What to do**

Starting at one side and working across, gather and staple each full width of cellophane into a 30 cm space so that it is gathered double. Gather and staple at the bottom too, possibly into the base of a display board or a piece of wood temporarily screwed in place for this purpose. Continue across the width of your wall, using different colours of cellophane. You could alternate two colours or use a range of colours.

Finish off each side with a row of giant coloured stars which can be fixed in place with loops of sellotape on the back.

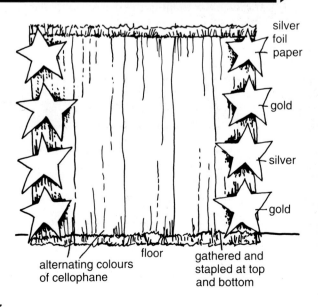

77

# ACTIVITY 5: DESERT NIGHT

**Materials needed**

Beige coloured corrugated card; green and brown ready-mixed paints; wall stapler; dark-coloured plain curtain (preferably blue); silver foil paper; straight pins or stapler.

**What to do**

Hang or staple the gathered curtain to the back wall.

Cut two pieces of card, each about 2 m × 1.5 m. Used card can be recycled if necessary. Draw a pencil outline of a pair of palm trees on each piece of card, then colour them by painting, sponging or rolling the paint. Each pair of trees should lean inwards. The trees can be cut out when dry and stapled to the wall and also attached to the edges of the curtain with straight pins or a stapler. Add a large cut-out silver star to complete the scene.

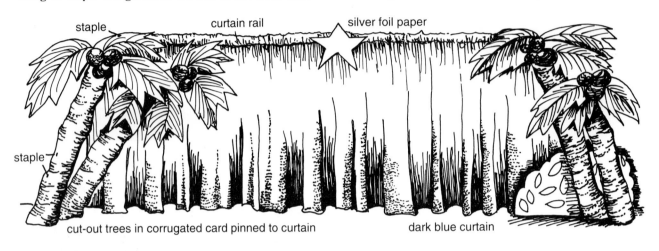

staple | curtain rail | silver foil paper

staple

cut-out trees in corrugated card pinned to curtain · dark blue curtain

# ACTIVITY 6: STARRY NIGHT

**Materials needed**

Corrugated card; 3 shades of blue paint or emulsion; large brushes or rollers; silver foil paper; white crêpe paper; wall stapler; thin card.

**What to do**

The corrugated card can be assembled as shown in three pieces if you have card backdrops that have been cut for previous use, or it can be cut as one complete piece, though the length makes this more difficult to handle if you are painting in a confined space. Mark the curved edges first with a pencil and then cut them out. Use a large brush or roller to fill in the shapes with different shades of blue, graduating from dark at the bottom to light at the top.

The card may stretch if moved when it is wet so allow

it to dry thoroughly overnight and then staple it in position for security. This is not a heavy backdrop so if your stage position has a window and curtain behind it, the card may be stapled or safety-pinned to closed curtains without causing damage.

For the stars, cut out about ten to twelve small stars (each 15 cm across) from silver foil and staple them to varying lengths of white crêpe paper which can be hung from the ceiling at the sides of the backdrop. If this is not possible, pin them to the curtain above the backdrop or stick them on to the backdrop with glue. The large star should be about 40 to 50 cm across for impact and needs to be glued to thin card for stability. Fix it just over the edge of the top curve of blue to give an impression of infinite height. The small stars may also need card backing to prevent them curling up.

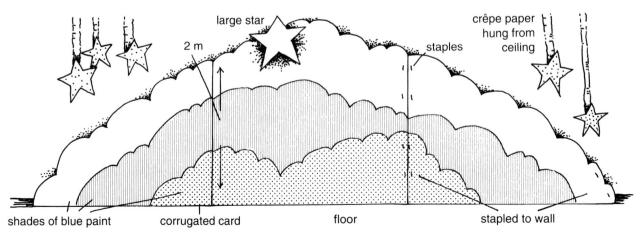

large star · crêpe paper hung from ceiling

2 m · staples

shades of blue paint · corrugated card · floor · stapled to wall

78

# ACTIVITY 7: WALLED STABLE

**Materials needed**
Large roll of corrugated card; 2 rectangular tables or cupboards or large cupboard boxes; black and grey paint; wall stapler; large brushes or sponge.

**What to do**
Use the plain face of the card as the front in this case so that it can be painted easily. Start by anchoring one edge of the card to a wall using staples (a), then anchor (b). The support can be almost anything which is about 1 m high and can stand up unsupported. A large cardboard box is quite adequate as it is held in place behind the card. You will need to fold the card quite sharply to make the pillar.

This backdrop needs to be painted *in situ* because of its size, so to minimise the risk of the card sagging with the wet paint, use the paint sparingly. Paint patches of stone effect with brushwork lines or use a large rectangular sponge to print the effect. Windows and doors can be painted with black outlines. A small spotlight can be used to highlight each section as needed, the central part being the stable.

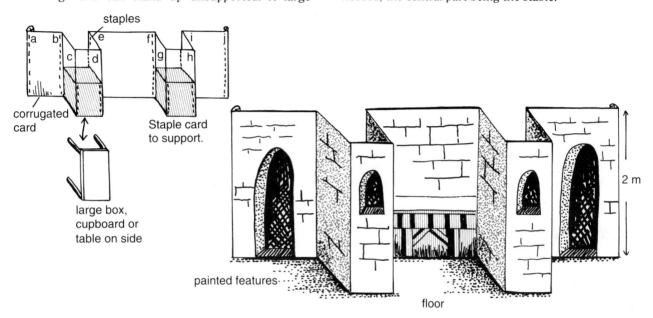

# ACTIVITY 8: SNOWY HILL

**Materials needed**
2 strong hooks; rawl plugs; 2 lengths of 5 cm × 2.5 cm wood or strong cane; green art paper; old white sheet or white paper or card; wall stapler; pale-blue ready-mixed paint; silver foil paper; PVA glue; large brushes.

**What to do**
This backdrop can be any size depending on materials available and indeed it can be successful even if a full-size bed sheet is used. It can be made from a sheet of card or paper, but care must be taken to ensure that paper doesn't tear. First of all staple the backdrop sheet to a wall or sellotape it stretched out on a table so that it can be painted. Use pale blue paint to outline the hills and to fill in the sky and then allow this to dry before gluing on a forest of small cut-out fir trees. Include two or three larger trees in the foreground to give depth to the scene. Cut out several stars from silver foil paper and glue on to the sky.

The medieval-style supports at the top of the backdrop are made from pieces of card 8 cm × 20 cm. These are folded, then stapled about 10 cm apart to the top reverse of the sheet. The wooden rod or cane is threaded through the loops and then hung on two strong hooks. A matching length of wood or cane is stapled to the bottom of the backdrop to weight it down.

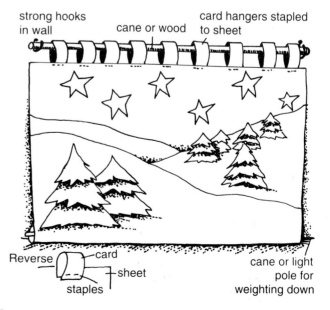

# ACTIVITY 9: FOREST

### Materials needed
Plain green curtain; green art paper; red foil paper; corrugated card; shades of green ready-mixed paint; staple gun; old sponge.

### What to do
Hang the gathered curtain on the back wall of the performance area. (See Activity 1 for ideas on hanging.) Now cut out about nine to twelve large holly leaves (each 50 cm long) from green art paper. Fold them down the centre, then open out again to give a 3D effect. Staple the leaves in threes, as shown in the illustration, with more groups on one side than the other so that you get a diagonal arrangement when the bushes are added. Make berries (15 cm diameter) from scrunched up pieces of red foil paper and add bunches to the centre of each group of leaves using staples, glue or sellotape loops.

For the bushes, cut out wavy bush shapes from corrugated card (1 m × 1 m approximate dimension), then decorate by painting the smooth side green. Add printed leaves using shapes cut from an old sponge. If your card is a shade of green, blue or brown there is no need to paint it before adding the leaves as these base colours will be effective with the leaf colour added. Staple the bushes to the wall and the curtain, placing two or three on the side with fewer holly leaves and one on the opposite side. You can also add footlight scenery (see Activity 14) to complete the forest.

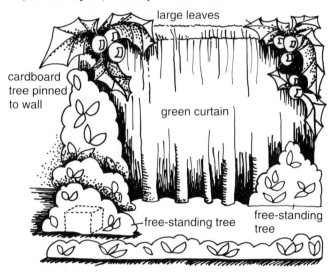

# ACTIVITY 10: PLAIN BACKDROP

### Materials needed
Corrugated card in a dark colour; staple gun; 2 rounders posts.

### What to do
Decide on the width of your backdrop and then add 2 m to the amount of card needed to allow for the curves to come out into the performance area.

Start by stapling one edge of the card to the back wall or to a piece of wood that can be screwed in place for this purpose. The two rounders posts can be positioned about 1 m out from the back wall and 1.5 m in from the side extent. Curve the card from its first anchor point and staple it to the first post. You will need to crease it along the whole length to hold the shape. Next curve the card in to touch the back wall. If possible staple it two or three times here to hold the shape, then curve it round the second post. Finally anchor the end of the roll to the opposite wall at stage right.

This backdrop provides a good plain focus for a variety of different performances.

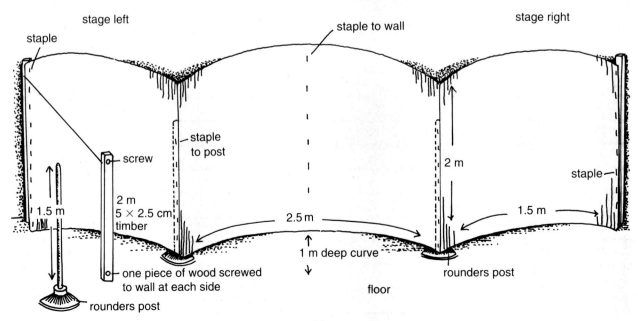

80

# ACTIVITY 11: HILLS TO STABLE

**Materials needed**

Light-coloured corrugated card; newspaper; white art paper; glue; silver foil paper; silver plastic foil; staple gun; assorted paints; large brushes, sponges and rollers.

**What to do**

Fix a length of corrugated card to the back wall of the performance area and on to this paint a simple outline of the inside of a stable, as shown. Black silhouette looks very effective.

To make the two doors, cut two pieces of corrugated card, both the same size as the back section, and fold each in half over a newspaper frame. Put a good amount of glue on one side of the frame before laying it on the

card, then fold the card over and staple the ends together. This stapled edge will form the hinge side of the door.

Each door can be painted with half of a very simple picture on each side: on the inside a black-outline eastern town and on the outside strips of sand, green hills and dark sky. When they are dry, staple the doors to either side of the backdrop. It isn't necessary for them to close completely or to meet exactly to create a feeling of mystery with the opening action.

Complete the scene with a large silver star and some plastic foil ribbon stapled to it as streamers.

The door facility is used as the action in the nativity play dictates, being fully open for the final tableau.

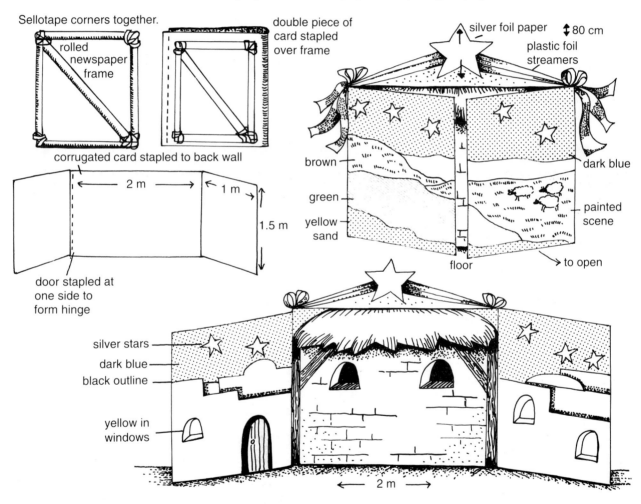

# ACTIVITY 12: SHOOTING STAR

**Materials needed**

Silver and gold foil paper; blue and silver flexible plastic foil or blue and yellow cellophane; black art paper or black-out curtain; white polyester or lining fabric; staple gun.

**What to do**

Cover the back wall of the performance site with sheets

of black art paper or a large black-out curtain. The tail of the shooting star can now be made from 2 m to 3 m lengths of plastic foil. If your rolls of foil are short you can join them by using sellotape on the back. Make four to six lengths of foil which will stretch diagonally across your backdrop and leave 1 m extra to hang down. Gather these into a bunch at one end, with colours alternating, and staple them very firmly to the stage right top corner. Now take each colour in turn and stretch it diagonally across, as shown, opening it to its fullest on the opposite end and then staple this in place. When each length is in place, take the remainder of the plastic foil that is left hanging, scrunch it up into a rough ball with a little left hanging down and staple the crumpled part in place.

Next you need to make two stars (one 80 cm and one 85 cm across) from gold and silver foil paper. Use one star as edging for the other. Staple them together over the start of the tail and the edge of the black backing.

To complete the backdrop, drape the white fabric in folds from the star to the lowest part of the tail and fix it in place with staples.

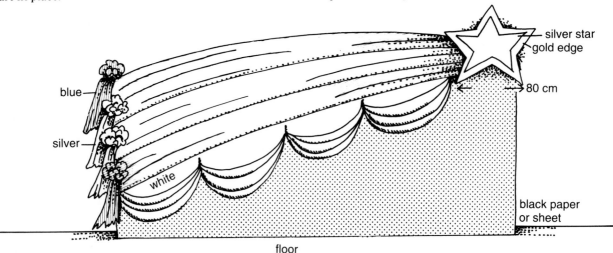

# ACTIVITY 13: WINGS

## Materials needed
Corrugated card; card; paint; staple gun; support, e.g. furniture.

## What to do
Decide first how far you need the wings to protrude from the side of the performance area and how high the structure needs to be to 'hide' performers waiting to come on. You will need to allocate a piece of furniture which is easy to move but stable enough to be placed behind the card base of the wings to support them. Many halls need to be cleared at lunchtime so the movable element of scenery is vital. If the furniture is moved then the card can be rolled back to the wall if necessary.

Simply cut a piece of corrugated card to the length and height required, tapering the side diagonally on longer wings to lead the eye to the main scene. Card should be painted when flat to prevent distortion. When decorating wings, a colour connection to the main scene is all that is required, with possibly a shape or two such as a few printed leaves or bricks. Attach the wings to a side wall with wide sellotape or staples.

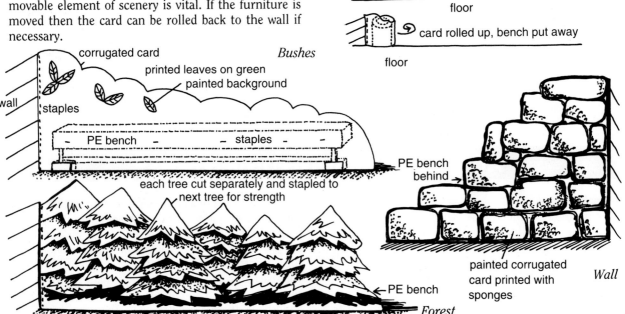

82

# ACTIVITY 14: FOOTLIGHTS

**Materials needed**
PE bench; front-of-stage blocks; staple gun; Blu-tack; corrugated card; assorted decorative paper; assorted paints; large brushes.

**What to do**
Some edging to the stage area is often useful to define the limits for the actors as well as looking more finished. Either the edge of the stage, if a raised area, or stage blocks can be used. A strip of corrugated card about 20 cm higher than the stage is needed. It can be fixed to its backing by sellotape loops, staples or, in some cases, Blu-tack. Steps can be masked by a piece of card of their own that is not attached to the main stage so that these can be stored when the hall is used for another activity. The card can be decorated in many ways and, as with wings, only a shape or a colour link to the main scene is needed, so this decoration need not be costly or time consuming to make.

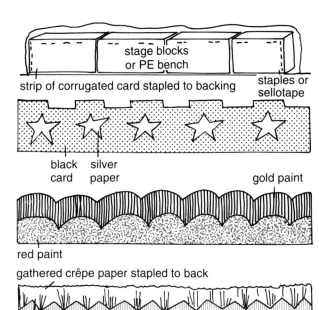

strip of corrugated card stapled to backing — stage blocks or PE bench — staples or sellotape

black card — silver paper — gold paint

red paint

gathered crêpe paper stapled to back

coloured card

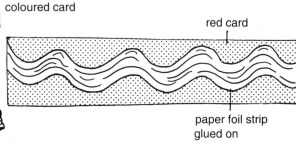

red card

paper foil strip glued on

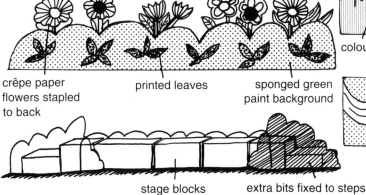

crêpe paper flowers stapled to back — printed leaves — sponged green paint background

stage blocks — extra bits fixed to steps

# ACTIVITY 15: BOX SCENERY: AN EASTERN TOWN

**Materials needed**
Sandy-coloured matt emulsion paint; large brushes; dark-grey ready-mixed paint; assortment of very large cardboard boxes.

**What to do**
Seal the smaller boxes securely with sellotape but try to stand larger boxes on their open ends so that the smaller ones can be stored inside them. Give each box one or two coats of sandy emulsion to obliterate any writing. If you have some paint a shade or two darker

you can lightly sponge blotches of darker paint over the lighter to give an impression of texture. Now, using the dark grey paint, draw on lines of stonework and windows and doorways in different shapes.

The boxes can then be used in a variety of combinations to build different scenes. For example, in a nativity play, they can be used as houses on the journey, the inn and the stable; they can be moved into different arrangements by stage hands during songs or other action. If stage hands wear dark clothes their actions rarely disturb.

TV/video box — washing-machine box — apple box — freezer box — TV box

# ACTIVITY 16: PROPS ROUND FURNITURE

**Materials needed**

Chairs, PE benches, piano, cupboards; staple gun; corrugated card; assorted paints; string.

**What to do**

Sometimes a performance may need scenery that can be climbed on by the actors to provide height for the action. For this purpose a low chair, a small stage block or a higher PE bench can be a stable base that can be disguised as scenery.

Larger items of furniture, such as cupboards, are difficult to relocate and in the case of a piano may be needed for the music. These too can be disguised as buildings and also provide useful wings.

Curtains can be hung around cupboards and pianos with permanent fixtures such as curtain wire and hooks. However, more imaginative coverings can be made from corrugated card cut and painted to create buildings, as shown in the illustrations. Higher scenery round the piano can also serve to hide a lamp on top which may be needed to provide light for the pianist in darker scenes.

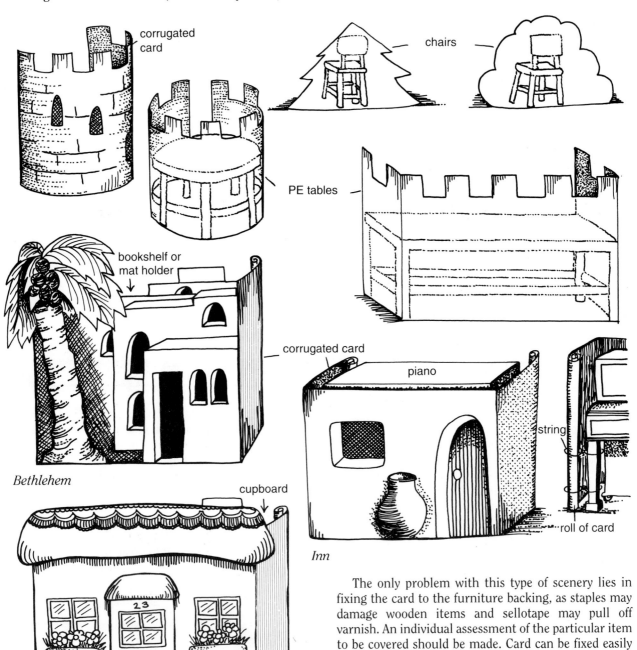

corrugated card

chairs

PE tables

bookshelf or mat holder

corrugated card

piano

string

roll of card

*Bethlehem*

cupboard

*Inn*

*Cottage*

The only problem with this type of scenery lies in fixing the card to the furniture backing, as staples may damage wooden items and sellotape may pull off varnish. An individual assessment of the particular item to be covered should be made. Card can be fixed easily and safely round metal legs and for good quality wooden furniture try rolling the edge of the card and using string to tie round piano legs and cupboard handles. Of course you will need to make sure that any string does not cause a hazard to footholds and that long robes do not interfere with any climbing.

# ACTIVITY 17: FREE-STANDING PROPS

**Materials needed**

Card; corrugated card; assorted cardboard boxes; assorted paints; sellotape or contact adhesive.

**What to do**

Draw small items of scenery such as bushes or cupboards and props such as stable animals, cooking pots or furniture on to large sheets of card or corrugated card. These can be painted and then either cut out completely round the shape or cut out with a smooth outline, like the ox shown here. The painted item is then fixed to a cardboard box support using sellotape or a good contact adhesive. It can be moved easily around the stage and because it is light can be stored on top of other scenery. Make sure that the support box is large enough to hold up the cut-out and also that any writing on the box is obliterated by a dark paint so that it is not visible on stage.

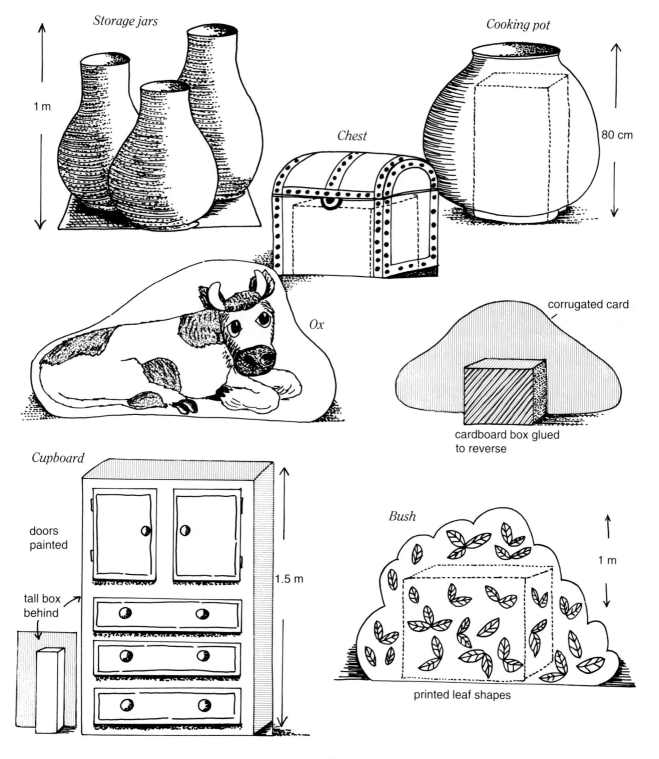

Storage jars

1 m

Cooking pot

Chest

80 cm

Ox

corrugated card

cardboard box glued
to reverse

Cupboard

doors
painted

tall box
behind

1.5 m

Bush

1 m

printed leaf shapes

# ACTIVITY 18: A MANGER

## Materials needed

2 apple boxes; brown and black ready-mixed paint; white or yellow cloth or blanket; newspaper; PVA glue.

## What to do

First of all sellotape the loose flaps to the inside of each box, then glue the two boxes together, bottom to bottom. Let this dry thoroughly, then paint the outside of the boxes brown. When this in turn is dry, paint arches in black, as shown in the illustration, to give the impression of legs on the manger. finally, pad the top box to half its depth with scrunched-up newspaper and lay the cloth or blanket inside with its edges draped over the top. The infant doll can now be put to bed, suitably wrapped in swaddling clothes.

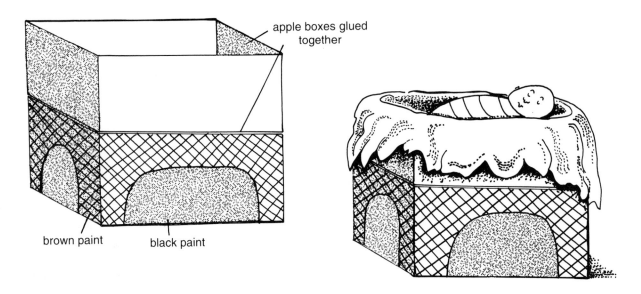

apple boxes glued together

brown paint          black paint

# ACTIVITY 19: DONKEY

## Materials needed

Card or brown art paper; brown crêpe paper; beige ready-mixed paint; white paper; brown sugar paper; paintbrushes; newspaper; Copydex adhesive; stapler.

## What to do

On the brown card or paper draw and cut out two simple donkey heads in the dimensions shown and two ears in the same material. Fold each ear in on itself at the bottom and staple this together. The ears can now be stapled to the inside of one of the head shapes, with one ear slightly lower than the other. On the right side of each head shape you now need to paint a beige-coloured semi-circular arch for the muzzle and add a black nostril with felt-tip pen. Draw and cut out large oval eye shapes on white paper and add pupils in black pen with a little triangle of white in each to provide a 'twinkle'. Glue these in position.

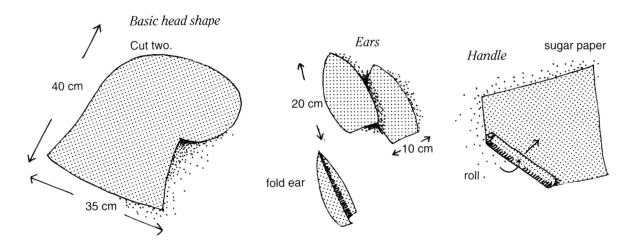

*Basic head shape*

Cut two.

40 cm

35 cm

*Ears*

20 cm

10 cm

fold ear

*Handle*

sugar paper

roll

For the donkey's mane cut a 10 cm wide strip from the whole length of a roll of brown crêpe paper and fringe it, leaving 2 cm at the bottom edge. Spread a thick line of Copydex to the top inside edge of one head side and stick the crêpe paper down along the glue, gathering it up to fit with generous tufts. The two halves of the head can now be stuck together with Copydex, leaving the bottom open for the time being.

The handle should be made next by rolling two sheets of brown sugar paper into a stick, starting on the diagonal. Roll up two more sheets over the lower part of the first to make the stick longer, fix the paper with sellotape and then trim it to about 1 m length.

The head needs a little filling out and this is done by gently pushing scrunched newspaper into the space inside. Sellotape the handle well up inside the head before sealing the bottom with staples or Copydex.

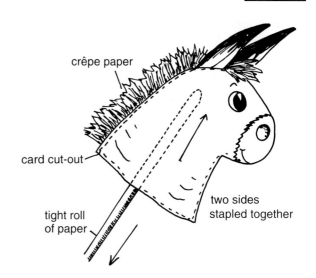

crêpe paper

card cut-out

tight roll of paper

two sides stapled together

# ACTIVITY 20: ANIMALS IN THE STABLE

**Materials needed**
Shades of brown and grey art paper; same shades of ready-mixed paint; large rectangular sponge; paintbrushes; staple gun.

**What to do**
Using a different shade of paper for each animal, draw large simple-shaped heads as shown in the illustration. Use fine brushes and brown shades of paint to add the features. You could also make a small crêpe paper fringe for the mane and glue it to the back of the donkey's head.

For the wall, select a suitable shade of art paper and use as many sheets as necessary, depending on the size you want the stable to be; the shape is simply stapled together. Use the sponge to print stone blocks either at random or in an all-over pattern, using different shades of brown paint. When you are assembling the stable let the front bell out very slightly to give a 3D effect. loops of sellotape can be used to fix the paper to a backing wall if staples are impractial. Slip the animal heads just behind the wall with their noses hanging over the edge a little and staple or sellotape them in place.

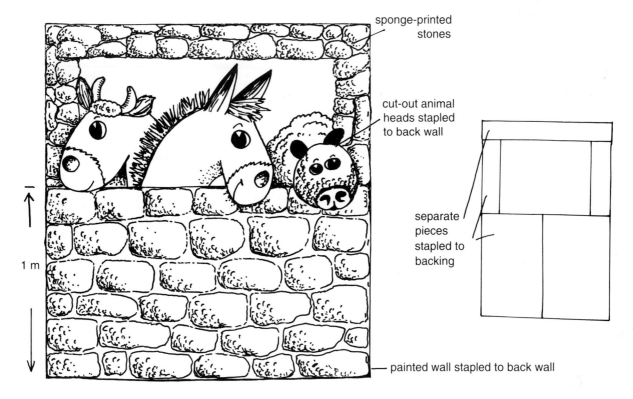

sponge-printed stones

cut-out animal heads stapled to back wall

separate pieces stapled to backing

1 m

painted wall stapled to back wall

# ACTIVITY 21: FREE-STANDING TREES

**Materials needed**

Rounders post; centre of carpet roll; card; corrugated card; paint; sponges; art paper in assorted colours; stapler; Copydex adhesive.

**What to do**

Cardboard centres of carpet rolls are usually too tough to cut with scissors or craft knieves and you may need a saw to cut them to the required length.

The rounders post will support a card roll quite well to about 30 cm above the height of the post, but any greater weight may overbalance it. Put the card roll on the post to paint it, first protecting the metal base with newspaper. Use any colour of ready-mixed paint, which should go on easily.

Three different types of tree are described, as shown in the illustrations.

For the deciduous tree, cut two pieces of card in the shape illustrated. Use brown or green card and sponge print leaf shapes on to it. Staple the two sides of the card together round the top curve, then use a staple gun and a good contact adhesive to fix this to the top of the roll.

For the palm tree, cut out palm leaves from green art paper. Make these about 90 cm long and fold them down the centre line to give a 3D effect. Fix about eight leaves in a bunch, using sellotape to bind them together, then smear the top inside of the card roll with a good contact adhesive and push the end of the bunch of leaves into this. Spread the leaves out to form a canopy.

For the fir tree cut out six simple fir tree shapes, about 1 m long, from green art paper. Fold each tree shape down the centre line and open it out. To fix the tree sections to the trunk, spread about two-thirds of the fold with a good contact adhesive and fix it to the trunk, with the top 30 cm extending over the top of the card roll. Continue round the trunk with the remainder of the tree sections, spacing them out equally.

As few as three trees of this type will look like a forest on stage. If you can put one tree on a stage block near the backdrop the height variation will give an impression of greater number.

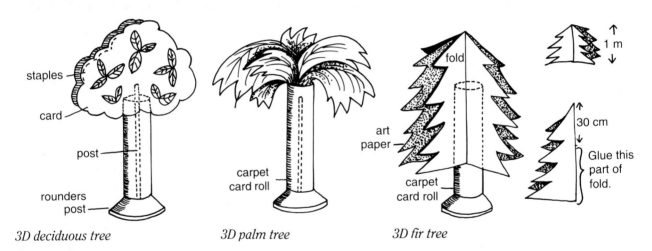

*3D deciduous tree*   *3D palm tree*   *3D fir tree*

# ACTIVITY 22: STICK PUPPET THEATRE

**Materials needed**

Cardboard box; coloured foil and cellophane papers; coloured card; Copydex adhesive; stapler; craft knife.

**What to do**

This type of table-top theatre is suitable for small card puppets on a stick. Puppets for the nativity story can be made simply by cutting out pictures of the characters from Christmas cards and sellotaping the base of each picture to a thin garden cane or a long stiff straw.

For the theatre you can select a box of any size that you feel suits the size of your puppets. It can be as small as a large shoe box or a food carton. First of all cut a rectangular hole bigger than the puppets on each side of the box; use a craft knife for this job which must be done by an adult. Again using the knife, cut a 1 cm wide slit, almost the length of the back, along the top back edge.

This is a slot for scenery, which merely consists of different pieces of card each with a scene painted on it. The card should be about 3 cm taller than the back of the theatre so that it can be handled easily.

An effective proscenium arch is made as follows. Turn the box on its side and sellotape the bottom flap back on itself to what now becomes the base of the theatre. Open out the other flaps as shown and cut a piece of card to fit over these flaps and round the opening of the box to form the proscenium arch. For a shoe box or any box without flaps leave 2 cm extra inside the arch and cut into the corners, then fold back the card and glue it on to the box to hold the arch in place. The arch can be decorated with coloured foil shapes or designs in felt-tip pen before it is fixed in place by gluing it to the flaps.

Puppets can be stored inside the theatre when it is not in use.

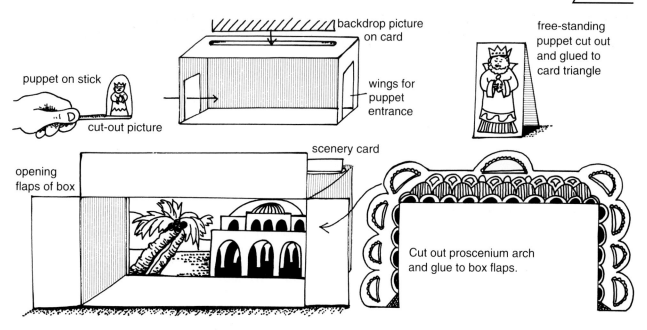

puppet on stick

cut-out picture

backdrop picture on card

wings for puppet entrance

free-standing puppet cut out and glued to card triangle

opening flaps of box

scenery card

Cut out proscenium arch and glue to box flaps.

# ACTIVITY 23: GLOVE PUPPET THEATRE

## Materials needed

Large cardboard box with 2 compartments, such as a fruit box; crêpe paper; assorted foil papers, glitter and ribbon; 2 tins with plastic lids; sand; assorted paints; stapler; glue; large brushes.

## What to do

This sort of theatre is used from the back and can stand on the floor or on a table. Stand the box in a vertical position and cut a proscenium arch in the top compartment. You may need to use a craft knife for this, in which case an adult should do it. You can now paint the theatre on the outside and leave the inside blank if it is unadorned by commercial markings.

To decorate the front of the theatre, add two curtains of crêpe paper which can be gathered with a stapler and then sellotaped in position. The join can be covered with a decoratively shaped piece of card making the top of the arch. This needs to be big enough to extend over the width of the hole and stand above the top of the box. It can be decorated with felt-tip pens or glued-on shapes of foil paper and then glued in position. For a special finishing touch you can cut out letters in foil paper for the theatre name and glue these to the front of the box.

The box will need to be weighed down for theatre use as exuberant activity can make it unstable. Fill two coffee tins or similar with sand and sellotape the lids in place. The tins can stand in the bottom of the box.

It is difficult to use a card backdrop in a theatre of this kind where the puppeteers need back access, so the best thing is to have a wide curtain to shield the 'back stage' area. Use a piece of self-coloured cloth which is at least 20 cm longer than the back opening and three times as wide. This will allow you to gather it at the top, either with staples or by using a needle and thread and then sellotaping the gathered section firmly on to the top of the box; let the curtain fall down over the open back. A good width of gather will allow the puppets easy access without exposing the puppeteers unduly.

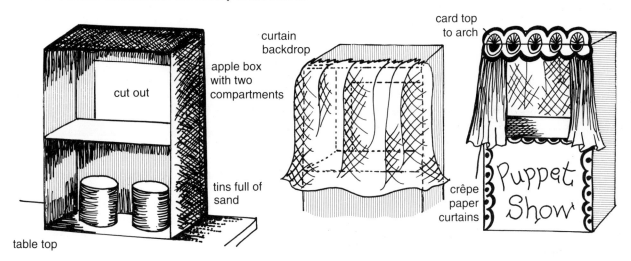

cut out

tins full of sand

table top

apple box with two compartments

curtain backdrop

card top to arch

crêpe paper curtains

Puppet Show

# HATS AND MASKS

## ACTIVITY 1: HAPPY FACE

**Materials needed**

Large paper plate; assorted scraps of art paper or foil paper; PVA glue; strips of wool or crêpe paper; A3 sheet of art paper; newspaper.

**What to do**

Start by marking the position of the eyes on the back of the paper plate. For the youngest children, take this opportunity to look at the way the features are positioned on the face: ears in line with eyes, nose on a central line, etc. Let them try out drawings on paper first and then help them to draw the eyes on the plate. These eye shapes can be cut out and the holes edged with a black felt-tip pen. To make the initial incision put the paper plate on a pad of newspaper and push the pointed end of the scissors through to the pad, then lift up the plate and continue the cutting from that starting point.

Now the face can be decorated to suit the tastes of the individual artist. It could be something completely different from the artist's own, perhaps with strange skin colours. This can be done with paint or with wax crayon. Other fantasy features can be added, but encourage the children to make smiling mouths for a party atmosphere. The features can be cut from scraps of art paper or foil paper and fixed in position with glue. For those children who have not yet developed good scissor skills, the adult can provide a selection of ready-cut pieces. Strips of wool or crêpe paper can be used for hair and fixed with glue or staples.

Finally, to make the handle, tightly roll a piece of A3 art paper diagonally from one corner and secure the end corner with a little sellotape. The ends can be clipped across with scissors to give strength and a neater appearance. The handle can be fixed with strips of sellotape to the back of the paper plate, positioning the top of the handle just under the eyes for greatest stability.

The 'wearer' of the mask holds it in front of their face like an eighteenth-century masquerade mask.

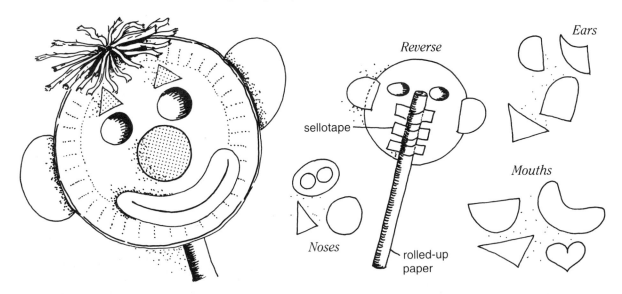

## ACTIVITY 2: STARS IN YOUR EYES

**Materials needed**

Stiff card; gold spray paint; silver and gold double-sided foil; small green garden stick; silver or gold foil parcel ribbon; PVA glue.

**What to do**

Cut out the basic mask shape as shown, bearing in mind that the position of the eye holes and the depth of the nose curve may need to be adapted to the individual. Older children will be able to do this themselves, using a pencil first to mark the eyes to allow for alterations. If required, the mask base can now be sprayed with gold paint, but remember that this should be done by an adult in a well-ventilated area. You may feel that older children can do this under supervision. Spray the sticks at the same time.

Each mask needs about 5 to 7 stars cut from double-sided foil. Make a five-point star template (about 6 cm wide); those children who are able to can use this to draw around and cut out their own stars. Arrange the stars along the top of the mask, slightly overlapping and alternating the colours. When a satisfactory design has been achieved, glue them in position. If you wish, strips of ribbon can be attached to the sides of the mask with staples or sellotape.

To complete the mask, sellotape the stick firmly to the back of one side, according to the dominant hand of the bearer.

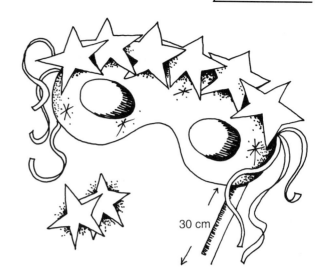

30 cm

# ACTIVITY 3: ROBIN CAP

## Materials needed
Black, white and red card; stapler; grey or brown tissue paper.

## What to do
Cut a strip of red card about 4 cm × 60 cm to make the circlet that fits round the widest part of the head. This circlet can be fitted to the individual and the ends stapled together to secure them.

Using white card, draw and cut out the eye shape. Colour the centre of the eyes with black felt-tip pen, leaving a little white triangle as the 'twinkle'. The eye shape can now be stapled to the front of the circlet, with a fan of grey or brown tissue paper between the eyes.

To make the beak, use black card for the shape. Fold the triangle down its length then open it out and fix it to the circlet with three staples, as shown.

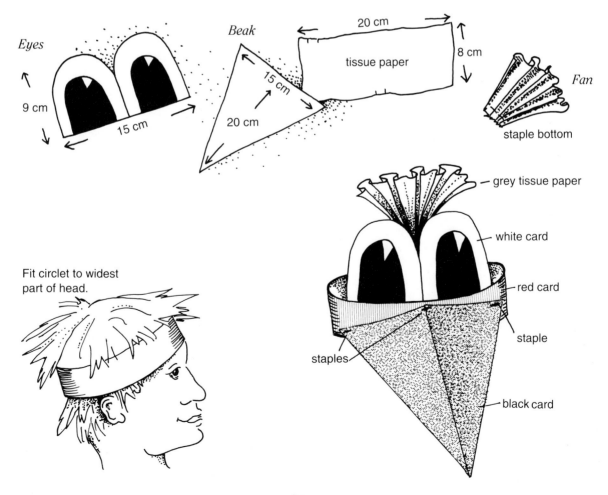

91

# ACTIVITY 4: GLITTERING EYES

**Materials needed**
Coloured cellophane; stapler; PVA glue; coloured glitter (to match the cellophane); black art paper; coloured plastic foil.

**What to do**
Make an eye mask with black art paper, as described for Activity 2. Then with an A3 piece of the same paper make a tight roll to use as a handle, which can be fixed in place with sellotape, as shown.

To decorate the mask make two frills in coloured cellophane, gathered at one end. These can be stapled to the sides of the mask near the top of the eyes. Add three 30 cm strips of plastic coloured foil to each side. Finally, to complete the decoration, carefully dribble glue over the front of the mask, avoiding the cellophane. Make swirls and curls with the glue and cover the staples too. Sprinkle glitter liberally over the glue and allow to dry before shaking off the surplus. The glue design will now be translated into a glittering one.

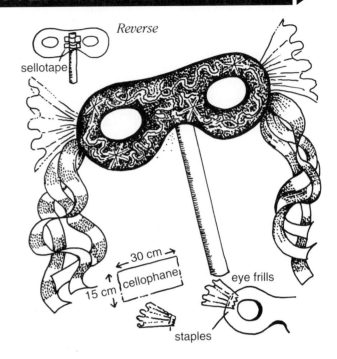

# ACTIVITY 5: CLOWN CAP

**Materials needed**
Coloured card: small white paper plate; scraps of coloured paper and foil; thick wool; PVA glue; ready-mixed paint.

**What to do**
Make a circlet of card to fit each child's head, as in the instructions for Activity 3. Now cut out an equilateral triangle from coloured card to use as the hat. A circle of coloured foil can be stuck on the end as a pom-pom and strips of wool stuck along the bottom of the triangle as hair.

The back of the paper plate is the face. It can be decorated by a variety of methods such as paint, cut-out pieces of paper or even scrap items like milk-bottle tops. You can provide ready cut-out shapes or allow the children to cut their own, depending on their range of skills. To include a little maths in the activity, you can use geometric shapes for the features, cut from foil paper, and talk about them.

To make up the cap, securely staple the top of the paper plate to the circlet, then staple the hat over the edge of the face. The circlet sits on the head like a visor.

# ACTIVITY 6: MONSTER TOP KNOT

**Materials needed**
White card; thick wool or crêpe paper; Copydex adhesive; clear plastic drinks bottle; stapler.

**What to do**
Make a circlet of card as described in Activity 3, using a strip about 60 cm × 4 cm, but do not staple it into a circlet yet as the next step is to make the hair. This can

be done in one of two ways. The first method is to cut strips of wool about 15 cm long and glue them side by side along the card strip. Encourage the children to work on a few centimetres at a time, applying glue, adding wool and repeating this process as they work along from left to right.

The second method is to cut a piece of crêpe paper about 120 cm × 15 cm, so that the grain of the crêpe

92

runs down the shortest length. Fold the strip in half and cut a fringe along it, leaving 4 cm at one side uncut so that it can be glued to the card circlet strip. This is quite a messy operation as the card strip should first be spread with glue and the crêpe paper then ruched evenly along its length. A backing strip of sellotape can be laid across this when the glue is thoroughly dry to prevent the Copydex rubber glue dragging at the wearer's hair.

The card and hair can now be made into a circlet by stapling it to the required size. It should be worn so that the hair comes from the inside and falls over the top.

The bouncing eyes are simple to make and provide an amusing feature. Cut a medium-sized plastic drinks bottle into 2 cm strips, as shown, then cut these into lengths of about 12 cm. Now cut two circles of white card, 6 cm in diameter, and draw pupils on them using black felt-tip pen and leaving a small triangle of the pupil white. Each eye is stapled to a plastic strip which in turn is stapled to the circlet on the inside and curling over the edge. As plastic bottles vary in thickness and consequently in springiness you may need to experiment before stapling the strips to the circlet, to adjust the length to maximum bounce.

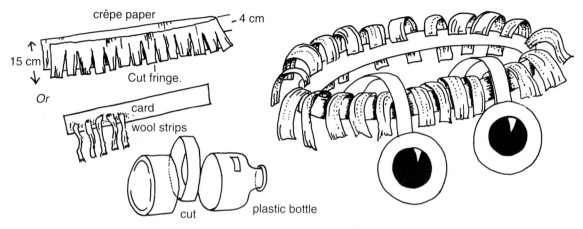

# ACTIVITY 7: RUDOLPH CAP

**Materials needed**
Brown, beige and white card; thick red wool; Copydex adhesive; stapler.

**What to do**
First of all you will need to make a circlet from the brown card, as described for Activity 3. You will also need to make the eye shape described in that activity, using white card and black felt-tip pen. Cut out two antler shapes from beige card; they should be about 12 cm long and about 6 cm across at the widest point. Then cut out two ears about 6 cm long from brown card. Staple, sellotape or glue all these features to the card circlet.

For Rudolph's nose, cut out a triangle of brown card, then round off the pint, so that the length is about 16 cm. Staple the nose to the circlet. The end of the nose is a woollen pom-pom, fixed to the brown card with a substantial blob of contact adhesive. Winding the pom-pom may be difficult, but it can be made a little easier if you cut the central hole in the card ring about 6 cm in diameter. The ultimate diameter of a pom-pom is the width of the winding space doubled. Small balls of wool are easier to hold while winding, so prepare small balls of about 2 m length for the children to use. All but the oldest children will need adult help to cut and bind the pom-pom. (Instructions for making a pom-pom can be found on page 48.)

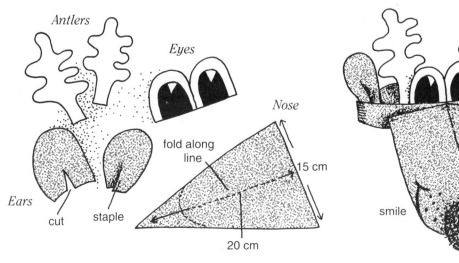

# ACTIVITY 8: FATHER CHRISTMAS HAT

### Materials needed
White card; cotton wool; red crêpe paper; Copydex adhesive; stapler.

### What to do
Prepare a circlet of white card, as shown in Activity 3. Cut a piece of red crêpe paper about 60 cm × 20 cm for the 'fabric' of the hat. Before stapling the circlet, run a strip of glue along it and stick the longer edge of the crêpe paper to this, gathering it slightly to fit if necessary. Now staple the circlet and join the open edge of the crêpe paper with tiny blobs of glue or staples. The top edge of the cap should be gathered together to a point and fixed with a rubber band or a staple. The join can be hidden with a large blob of cotton wool glued over the end to form a pom-pom. Finally, glue a strip of cotton wool or separate pieces, round the outside edge of the card to hide the join of the paper and make the white edge of the hat.

The beard is cut from white card. The size can be adjusted to suit individuals by varying the depth of the inner part cut out for the face. The beard can be decorated either by cutting a fringe in the bottom or by covering it with a fine layer of cotton wool. To do this, spread a small part of the beard at a time with glue and then tease out a piece of cotton wool to its thinnest before putting it gently on the glue. Another alternative is to decorate the beard with fringes of crêpe paper. When the beard is finished, staple it to the circlet.

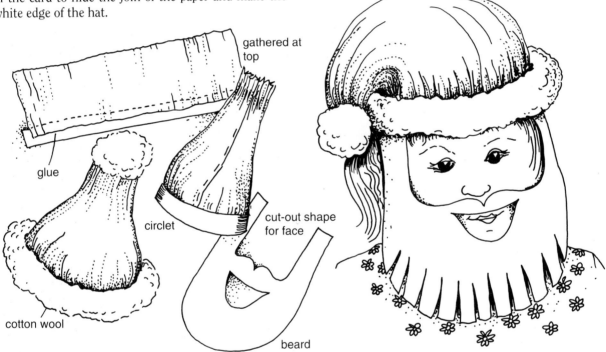

gathered at top

glue

circlet

cut-out shape for face

cotton wool

beard

# ACTIVITY 9: FESTIVE GARLAND

### Materials needed
White or red card; green double-sided foil or green art paper; red foil paper; green and red foil parcel ribbon; stapler; glue.

### What to do
Make a circlet of card as shown in Activity 3, using either red or white card. Cut six strips of coloured ribbon, each about 40 cm in length. Curl the ends of the ribbon by holding a pair of scissors between finger and thumb and pulling the ribbon through against the scissors. Staple the ribbons at one end in two sets of three.

Position the garland by putting the circlet, at this stage joined temporarily by a paper clip, on the wearer's head. Sellotape the two bunches of ribbon in place, one on each side just over the ears. They can be fixed to the outside of the circlet and holly leaves glued over them to hide the join.

You may need as many as fifteen holly leaves and the same number of red berries. If you prepare a template, several leaves can be cut out at once, as shown. Glue the leaves on the circlet in pairs or fours and place about three berries in the centre. This can be done with the card circlet flattened out. Finally, staple the circlet together and add a couple of leaves to cover the join.

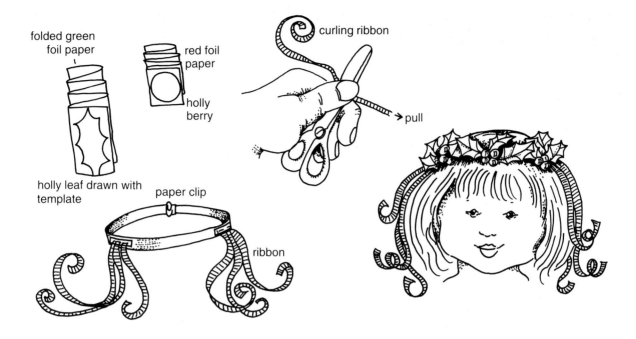

folded green
foil paper

red foil
paper

holly
berry

curling ribbon

→ pull

holly leaf drawn with
template

paper clip

ribbon

# ACTIVITY 10: SNOWFLAKE HEADBAND ▶

**Materials needed**

Old plastic head-band; white crêpe paper; white cartridge paper; silver plastic foil; Copydex adhesive.

**What to do**

To begin with, the head-band must be covered with silver to provide a base for the snowflakes. Cut a 2 cm wide strip of plastic silver foil. Sellotape one end of the strip to one end of the head-band, then wind the foil tightly round the band to cover it and secure with sellotape at the other end. You will probably need about 50 cm of foil. If you haven't enough head-bands an alternative can be made with a 2 cm wide circlet of white card, as described in Activity 3; the card can be left white.

Next cut six lengths of white crêpe paper and two lengths of plastic silver foil, each about 50 cm long and 3 cm wide. Staple together three white strips and one foil strip and sellotape one bunch at each end of the head-band. If you are using a card circlet, staple one bunch on each side just above the wearer's ears.

Finally, the snowflakes! Cut out about six 6 cm diameter circles of white paper. Fold each circle into six, then cut out shapes along the edges through the layers. Open the circles out again to reveal the snowflakes. Small sharp scissors are needed for snowflakes as tiny as these, but with care this can be attempted by Key Stage 1 children with good hand control. The snowflakes are fixed in a row across the head-band with a small blob of Copydex adhesive. Place one snowflake over the spot where the ribbons are joined on each side and space out the other snowflakes across the band.

cuts

circle folded
into six

foil wound round
head-band

staple

strips of crêpe paper
and plastic silver foil

# ACTIVITY 11: ST LUCIA CROWN

**Materials needed**

Green and white card; gold and green foil paper; green art paper; Copydex adhesive; stapler.

**What to do**

Make a circlet of green card as described in Activity 3, but don't staple it together yet. Cut out seven candles, 10 cm × 3 cm, from white card and glue a small gold foil flame shape to the top of each. The candles can be fixed to the green card strip using a stapler. Even the youngest children can be helped to use this quick fixing aid. Space the candles out evenly and make sure the flames are all showing on the same side. The candles can overlap the front of the card as they will be covered up with leaves.

You now need to cut out about twenty leaves, some from art paper and some from green foil. Fold a strip of paper and cut out several leaves at once. The leaves can be glued around the circlet, covering the ends of the candles and the staples and overlapping each other. The foil leaves can be evenly spaced amongst the others to give a sparkle. Finally, staple the back of the circlet together and add a couple of leaves over the join.

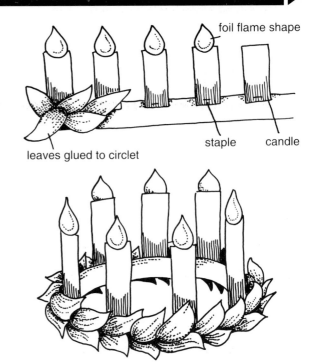

foil flame shape

leaves glued to circlet

staple    candle

# ACTIVITY 12: MONKEY MASK

**Materials needed**

2 large white paper plates; black card; dark-brown and light-brown ready-mixed paint; thick brown wool; stapler.

**What to do**

This mask is to be worn over the face, not as a visor, so you will need to fit it to the individual. Cut a strip of black card about 3 cm × 50 cm for the strap to hold the mask in place. Staple this 4–5 cm in from the edge of the plate on one side only. Now hold the plate against the wearer's face and fit the card strap round the back of the head slightly above the widest point so that it has a secure fit. Mark the place then remove the mask and staple the other end of the strap in position, again

4–5 cm in from the edge. Sit the mask on the head again to mark the position of the eyes with a pencil. An adult can cut out the eye holes or older children can do it themselves.

You will now need to paint this plate dark brown and the second plate light brown. When they are both dry, cut the light brown plate in half. Shape one half as shown for the muzzle and cut two large ears from the second half. Use a black felt-tip pen to edge the eye holes and draw arched eyebrows. Some strands of dark brown wool can be stapled or glued to the top as a tuft of hair. Draw a smiling mouth and two nostrils on the muzzle and staple it on to the bottom of the face, slightly belled out (stapled 1 cm in from each side) to give a 3D effect. Staple the ears in position to complete the mask.

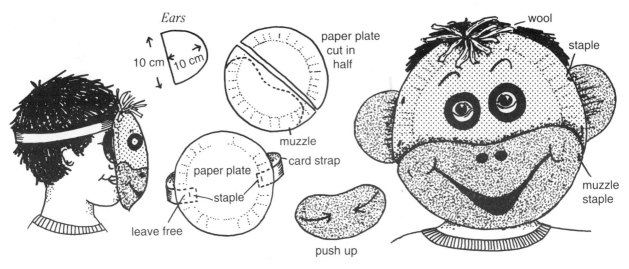

*Ears*

10 cm  10 cm

paper plate cut in half

muzzle

card strap

paper plate

staple

leave free

push up

wool

staple

muzzle staple

# ACTIVITY 13: KING OF THE JUNGLE

## Materials needed

Large white paper plate; black card; yellow and brown ready-mixed paint; yellow and orange crêpe paper; Copydex adhesive; black paper; yellow paper; 3 art straws; stapler.

## What to do

This mask is similar in structure to the Monkey Mask so begin by fitting the strap and cutting the eye holes in the same way. The face of the lion can then be painted in a yellowy-brown colour and left to dry. Next prepare the features. Paint three art straws black, cut out a nose in black paper and two ears in yellow paper. The latter can be glued in position before the mane is done.

For the mane, you will need 1 m each of yellow and orange crêpe paper, each in a strip 8 cm wide. While it is still on the roll, it is useful to cut the paper into as many 8 cm strips as you can, then cut fringes in the smaller rolls before opening them out. Turn the mask on to its face. Spread about 10 cm at a time with glue and gather one strip of crêpe paper on to it, working round the edge of the plate. Repeat this with the other strip of crêpe, gluing it a little nearer to the edge. The fringes will open out and show both colours.

The features can now be added. Edge round the eyes with black felt-tip pen and draw eyebrows. Glue the nose in position and draw a black muzzle. The painted straws can be cut in half and fixed to the muzzle with a little glue to complete the mask.

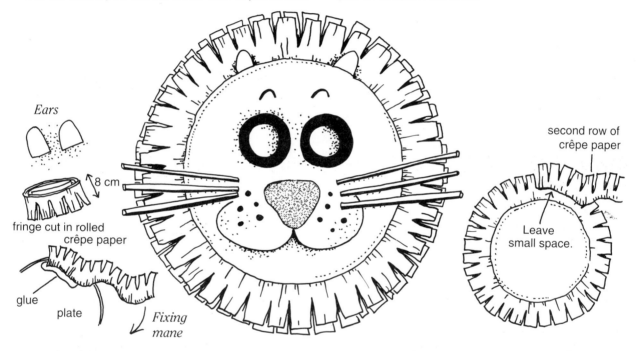

*Ears*

8 cm

fringe cut in rolled crêpe paper

glue

plate

*Fixing mane*

second row of crêpe paper

Leave small space.

# ACTIVITY 14: SPACEMAN

## Materials needed

White card (about 60 cm × 30 cm); Copydex adhesive; assorted small plastic lids and container tops; metallic spray paint; cellophane; pipe-cleaners.

## What to do

Make the basic cylinder as for Activity 15, but cut the eye hole larger as a half-face-size panel with curved corners. Cut a slight curve on the bottom of the cylinder to fit to the curve of the wearer's shoulder. You can now add an assortment of small bottle tops and lids to the outside of the helmet to represent dials and valves, using Copydex or another good contact adhesive to fix them in place. (Larger lids will be difficult to fit to the curve of the cylinder.) The cylinder with its decorations can now be sprayed with metallic paint. When it is dry, fix a sheet of clear acetate or cellophane to the inside of the face panel. Coloured pipe-cleaners can be sellotaped to the top edge as aerials.

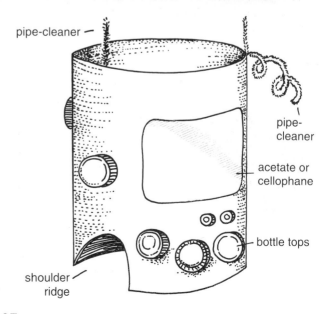

pipe-cleaner

pipe-cleaner

acetate or cellophane

bottle tops

shoulder ridge

97

# ACTIVITY 15: ALIEN FORCE

## Materials needed

White card (about 60 cm × 30 cm); coloured or glittered pipe-cleaners; cellophane; 2 automatic-washing-machine plastic powder globes; cotton wool balls; stapler; Copydex adhesive; PVA glue; ready-mixed paint.

## What to do

Shape the card into a cylinder which will sit comfortably over the wearer's head like a knight's helmet and staple or sellotape the edges together. Mark the position of the eyes with a pencil, then remove the helmet and draw a mouth shape over the position of the eyes; this will become the viewing hole. The shape can be anything the artist feels suitable, then cut out.

Now the outside of the cylinder can be painted with a mixture of PVA glue and ready-mixed paint (one to one ratio) in any pattern and colour. Alternatively, it can be sprayed with a metallic paint or marbled (see p. 34).

When this is dry you can move on to the adventurous part of the decoration. Cut a piece of cellophane larger than the mouth hole and glue this inside the cylinder at the back of the hole to camouflage the eyes as they peer out. Long sparkling pipe-cleaners can be added all over as feelers or hairs. To do this, simply make a very small hole in the card with the sharp point of the scissors, push about 2 cm of the pipe-cleaner through the hole, bend it to sit flat against the card wall and secure it in position with sellotape. Add blobs of coloured cotton wool balls between the pipe-cleaners, fixed with a little glue. Finally, add the two large washing powder globes for eyes. These may need a good bed of Copydex or another contact adhesive or even 'hot glue gun'. The latter should be used only by an adult; remember that the glue is twice the temperature of boiling water at point of exit, so great care must be taken with safety precautions.

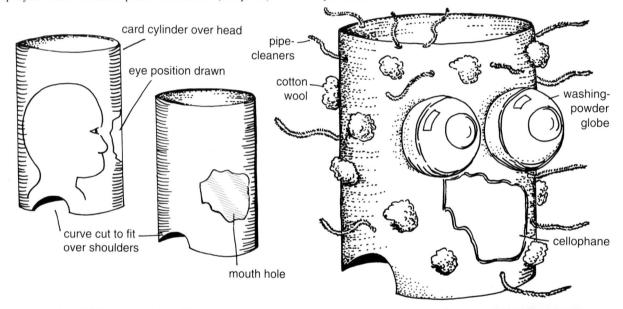

card cylinder over head

eye position drawn

curve cut to fit over shoulders

mouth hole

pipe-cleaners

cotton wool

washing-powder globe

cellophane

# ACTIVITY 16: A CHRISTMAS GIFT

## Materials needed

Small cardboard box; wrapping paper; foil parcel ribbon; strip of card (2 cm × 60 cm); Copydex adhesive.

## What to do

Make a circlet from the strip of card and fit it to the widest part of the head. Staple the ends together. This band will be used as a template for the size of the hole to be cut in the box. Alternatively, make the circlet to fit the back of the head so that the box is worn like a pill-box hat.

Put the circlet on top of one side of the box (not the open end) and carefully draw around it, trying to keep the shape. The hole can then be cut out on the inside of the line to allow for any adjustments and the open edges of the box sellotaped closed. Sit the box on the wearer and cut the hole larger if necessary. Now wrap the box as a parcel, ignoring the hole but using this side as the bottom of the parcel. Sellotape the wrapping paper in place securely as you would for a gift.

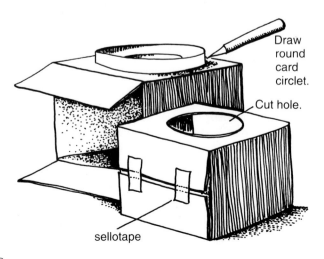

Draw round card circlet.

Cut hole.

sellotape

You now need to expose the head hole and secure the wrapping paper inside it. To do this, hold the box firmly in one arm with the base uppermost and break carefully into the paper in the centre of the hole. Cut from the centre to the edges so that the paper is cut like slices of cake or spokes on a wheel, then trim the point off each piece. Spread Copydex on the inside of each of these pieces and fold each strip back into the hole, fitting it to the curve and pressing it firmly in place.

Finally, the parcel needs a ribbon. Cut four pieces of ribbon, each about 50 cm long. Sellotape one end of each piece inside the head hole, then pull them up and tie in a bow on the top of the parcel. The gift is now ready to be worn on the head as a hat. For the pill-box style add an elastic chin strap.

Sellotape ribbons in hole and tie on top.

# ACTIVITY 17: MOUSE EARS

### Materials needed
Round balloon; card; scrap white paper; grey or white elastic; PVA glue; grey ready-mixed paint; thick black wool; red or pink crêpe paper if making bow.

### What to do
Blow up the balloon and tie the end. For easy handling you can secure the balloon to the edge of a table, as shown in the illustration. Cut up about twenty sheets of scrap A4 paper into strips roughly 2 cm × 10 cm. Paste each one individually with glue and lay them across the top half of the balloon in a single criss-crossed layer. Let this dry then add at least four more layers, with the strips going in different directions each time to give a strong structure.

Now cut out two ear shapes in firm card. Fringe the lower edge, as shown, and glue them to the top of the

cap, curving each ear in towards itself to give a realistic shape. Cover the join, the ears and the rest of the cap with another layer of paper strips and leave to dry thoroughly.

While the balloon and the cap are still supported, paint the cap with a mixture of grey paint and PVA glue (one to one ratio). A darker grey colour inside the ears will give them added shape. The artist can now enjoy popping the balloon base, then the edge of the paper cap can be trimmed with scissors. If you wish, the inside of the cap can be painted at this stage.

Add a chin strap of grey or white elastic, with the ends stapled to the cap or tied through a hole in each side. For a final touch, staple a tuft of thick black wool to the front of the cap and, for 'lady' mice, add a crêpe paper bow in red or pink. This can be glued in place over the tuft of wool.

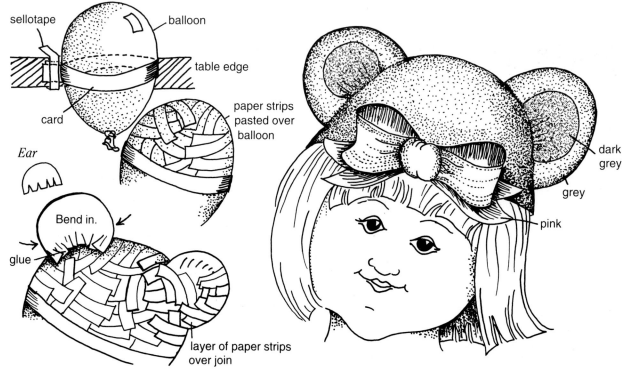

99

# ACTIVITY 18: CHRISTMAS PUDDING

## Materials needed

Round balloon; card; scrap white paper; circle of card about 30 cm diameter; brown, black, yellow and red ready-mixed paint; PVA glue; green and red art paper; 2 paper doilies; Contact or Fablon; black elastic.

## What to do

Make the cap as described in Activity 17 and paint it with a mixture of PVA glue and paint (one to one ratio) in a medium brown colour. When this is dry add some dots of black and dark yellow paint to represent currants and other fruit. Remove the balloon base and trim the edge of the cap.

To make the plate, sit the cap on the circle of card and draw round the base with a pencil. Cut out the centre a little inside the line to give a good fit and pull the card over the pudding, cutting slits if necessary in the plate. To secure the cap to the plate on the inside, use a strip of sticky-backed plastic like Contact or Fablon (white or clear) as this is more flexible than sellotape; the strip can be run all round the inside circle then folded over the edge of the plate.

To add a festive finishing touch, cut out two holly leaves and three berries from art paper and fix to the top of the pudding with a little glue. To disguise the join of the plate and the pudding add several bunches of holly leaves all round the edge of the plate or a strip of white paper doily. For the latter, cut the centre pattern from two large doilies and pull out the remaining edge to make a wavy strip which can be lightly glued in place.

Add a chin strap of black elastic as for Activity 17.

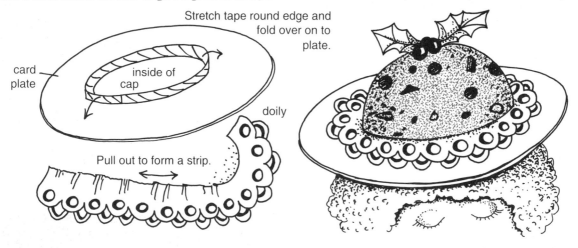

Stretch tape round edge and fold over on to plate.

card plate

inside of cap

Pull out to form a strip.

doily

# ACTIVITY 19: GIANT SWEETIE

## Materials needed

Round balloon; card; scrap white paper; PVA glue; coloured cellophane (approx. 60 cm × 90 cm); coloured foil paper; ready-mixed paint in any colour; white elastic.

## What to do

Make the cap as described in Activity 17 and paint it any bright colour you choose. Attach the elastic chin strap. Cut out ten circles of coloured foil about 3 cm in diameter and glue these all over the top of the cap.

To add the cellophane cover to the sweet, sellotape the shorter sides of the cellophane to the front and back of the cap, then gather up a bunch of cellophane at each side and secure with a strip of sellotape. You can then turn the cap on its back and pull the edges of cellophane over the edge of the cap and secure them on the inside with strips of sellotape. Tease out the two bunches of cellophane and the giant sweetie is ready to wear.

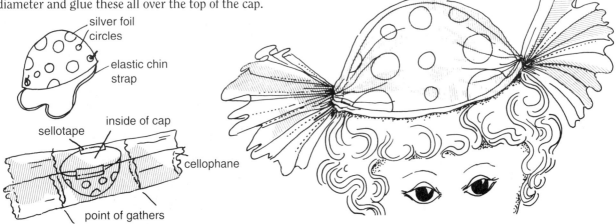

silver foil circles

elastic chin strap

inside of cap

sellotape

cellophane

point of gathers

# ACTIVITY 20: FESTIVE BIRD

## Materials needed
Round balloon; card; scrap white paper; assorted colours of stiff art paper; white paper; stapler; ready-mixed paint; PVA glue; brown or black elastic; Copydex adhesive.

## What to do
Make the cap as described in Activity 17 and paint the body of the bird in whatever colour you wish. For example, use brown for a robin and add a red semi-circle for its breast. Use PVA glue mixed with paint (one to one ratio) for a durable and pliable finish. Attach the elastic chin strap.

For the beak cut a 15 cm equilateral triangle out of art paper, fold it down the centre to give a 3D appearance and fix to the edge of the cap with a little Copydex. Cut out two eyes from white paper and add pupils with black felt-tip pen. Slip these side by side under the top of the beak before the glue dries and bend them forward slightly so that they stand up.

To make the wings and tail, cut three pieces of art paper, 22 cm × 14 cm, and fold each into a fan along the shorter side, with folds about 1 cm wide. Staple each fan about 2 cm from the end. An adult will need to cut three slits in each cap with a craft knife so that the fans can be secured in place. For the wings cut horizontal slits about 1.5 cm long and about 3 cm from the bottom. For the tail cut a vertical slit in the middle of the back at about the same height. Push the fans into the slits and sellotape the ends flat to the inside of the cap. You may need to spread out the tail fan and staple each side in this opened position to the cap.

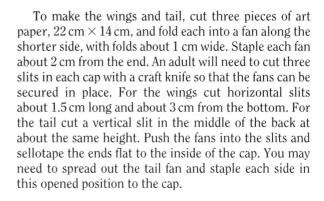

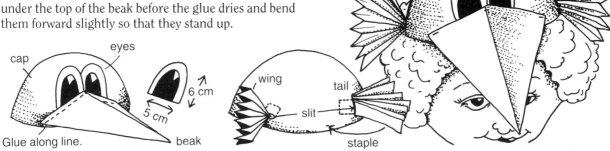

# ACTIVITY 21: CHRISTMAS TREE HAT

## Materials needed
Semi-circle of green art paper (50 cm diameter circle); green crêpe paper; assorted colours of foil paper; assorted colours of tissue paper scraps; black elastic; stapler; Copydex adhesive.

## What to do
Shape the green paper semi-circle into a cone that fits the wearer's head and secure it with a staple, then run a strip of sellotape down the join. Cut the crêpe paper roll into 4 cm strips while still on the roll, then cut fringes in the smaller rolls to a depth of 2.5 cm. This is to be wound round the cone to make the foliage on the tree. Secure one end of one of the rolls to the top of the cone with a little glue, then let the rest drop and wind it closely in a spiral as far down as it will go. Join another

roll on with glue and roll this to the bottom of the cone, securing the end with glue. You may need to keep the crêpe paper in place with little dots of glue as you wind it round.

Cut out an assortment of different-sized circles in various colours of foil. Cover the backs of the circles with Copydex and stick them on top of the crêpe paper, evenly spaced. The glue should soak through the crêpe and secure it to the cone. Take small scraps of coloured tissue and screw them into balls, then with a dot of glue place them between the foil circles.

Cut out two stars of equal size in silver foil and glue them back to back on the point of the tree to complete the decoration. Add a chin strap of black elastic, securing it to the hat with staples.

101

## COPYMASTERS

### 1: Stable outline
This can be enlarged to make a backdrop for a puppet theatre. The children could also draw figures on it or stick on cut-out figures to produce a picture or a Christmas card.

### 2: Roofscape
This sheet can be used as a background for a cut-out of Santa on his sleigh, or he can be drawn in the sky or on the roof-top.

### 3: Countryside
This can be photocopied to A3 size and the figures from Copymaster 8 coloured, cut out and stuck on with a small bracket of card to give a 3D effect.

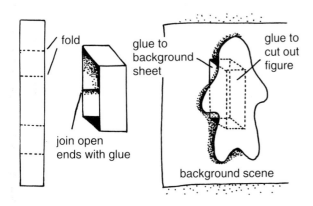

### 4,5: Templates of star, holly leaf, bell and ribbon
These templates can be photocopied to any size, then cut out and drawn round on art paper. Such shapes can form a useful part of any festive display: for example, two stars and a collection of holly leaves could be stuck on a corner of a display board or the shapes could provide a frame round a title.

### 6: Father Christmas in his sleigh
This can be coloured and glitter can be added (spread a small amount of PVA glue where required and sprinkle glitter over it). It can form part of a collage picture of a town on Christmas Eve or it can be used as a Christmas card.

### 7: Father Christmas mask
This can be photocopied on to card and cut out. The features and hat can be coloured with felt-tip pens, then cotton wool or glitter glued on to the beard and hair.

To make a face mask, cut out the eyes and attach a piece of thin elastic to go round the wearer's head.

### 8: Figures for a winter scene
The figures can be coloured and cut out then fixed to a painted or fabric collage background. (Copymaster 3 can be used as a background.)

Each figure could be enlarged to whatever size is required, cut out and used as a base for collage with paper, paint, scraps of fabric and other items.

### 9–13: Puppet theatre backdrops
 9. Kitchen
10. Ballroom or throne room, or rich person's house
11. Forest, woodland or garden
12. Bethlehem
13. Garden or park

These can be used as backdrops to puppet theatres and for this purpose can be coloured with felt-tip pens or painted. They can also be used as a base for children's own drawings of figures which can be cut out and glued on either flat or belled out slightly to give a 3D effect.

### 14: Greetings
This can be filled in with coloured pens or glitter and used as part of a Christmas card. It can also be enlarged to A3 size for use in a wall display.

### 15 and 16: Happy New Year and Happy Christmas
These sheets can be used in a similar way to Copymaster 16, enlarged or reduced as required.

### 17: Template for a square pyramid
The template can be decorated and then cut out to form this 3D shape. With the addition of a little ribbon, it can be used as a decoration.

It can also be photocopied on to thin card or laid on top of card and the lines drawn over heavily with a pencil to transfer the impression. The card shape can be made into a gift box by leaving one triangular side unglued as a lid.

Several pyramids can be glued together to form a variety of multi-sided shapes. They can be sprayed with gold paint, and gold ribbon used to suspend them as decorations.

### 18: Template for a cube
This can be treated in the same way as Copymaster 17. Both can be enlarged as required.

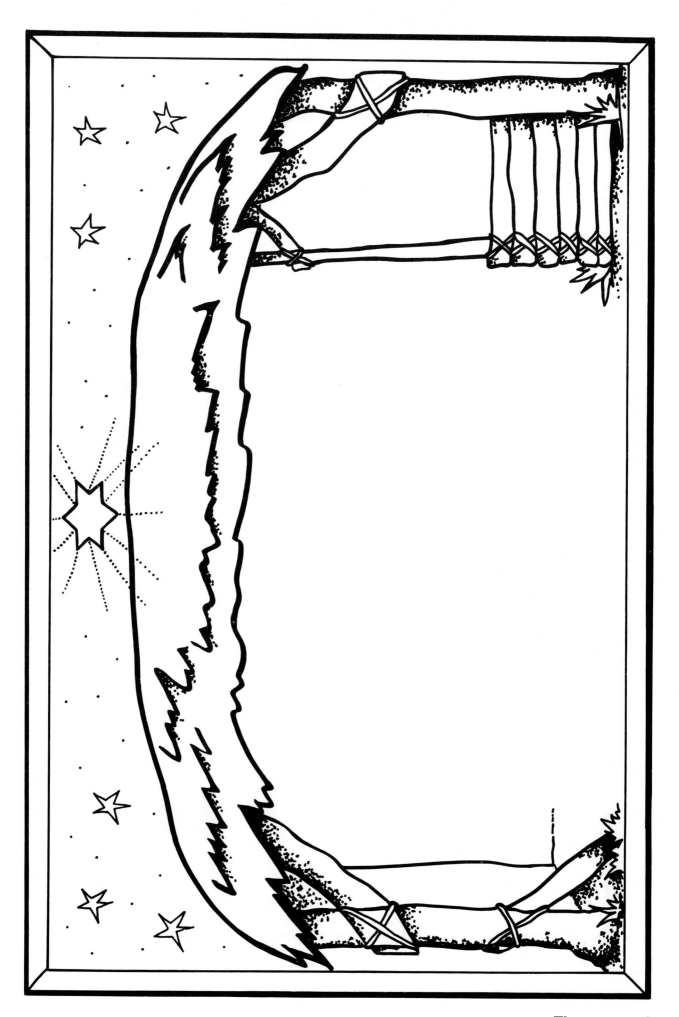

Timesavers 1

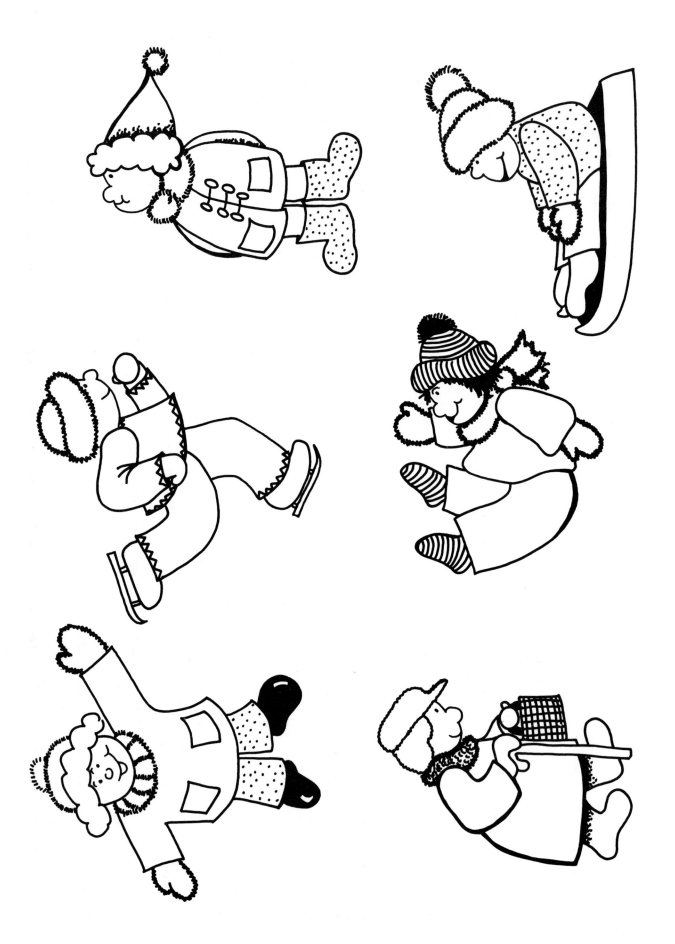

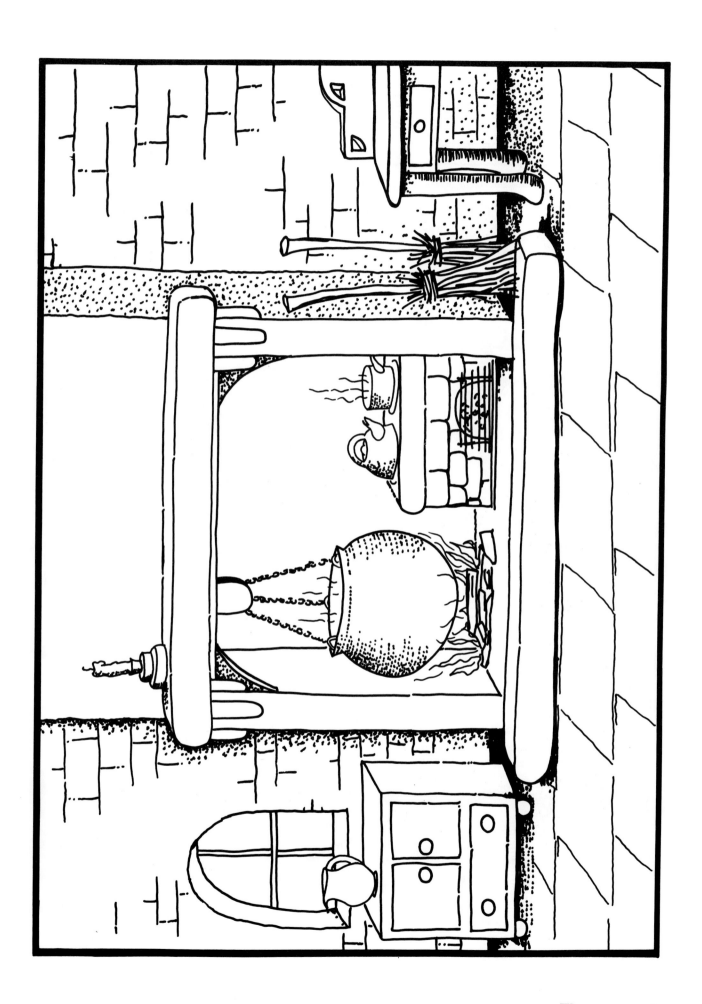

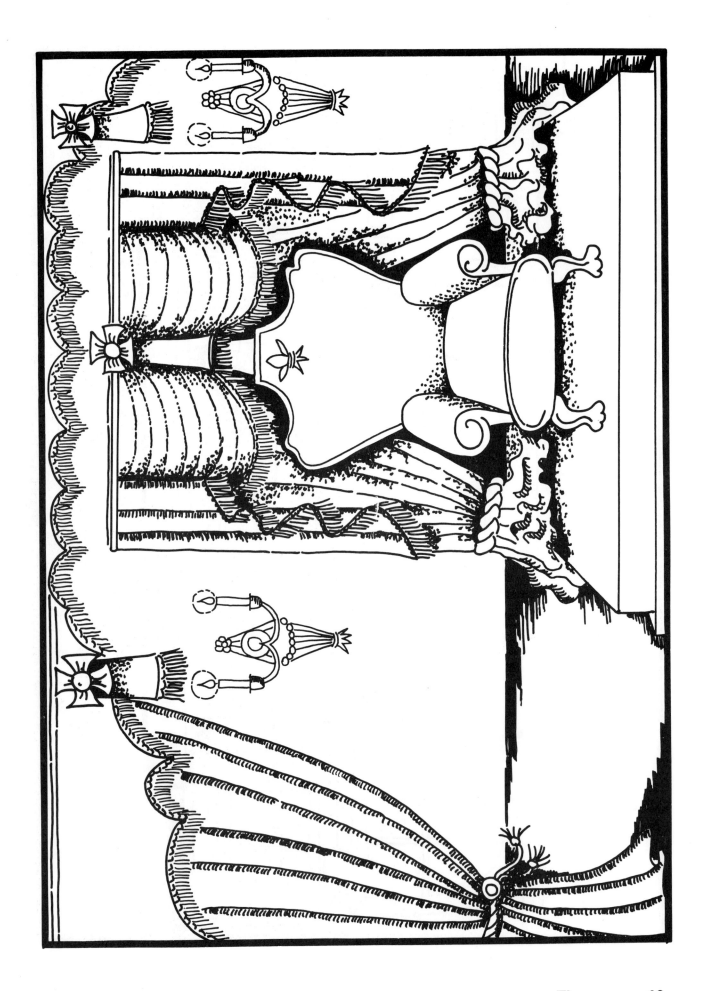

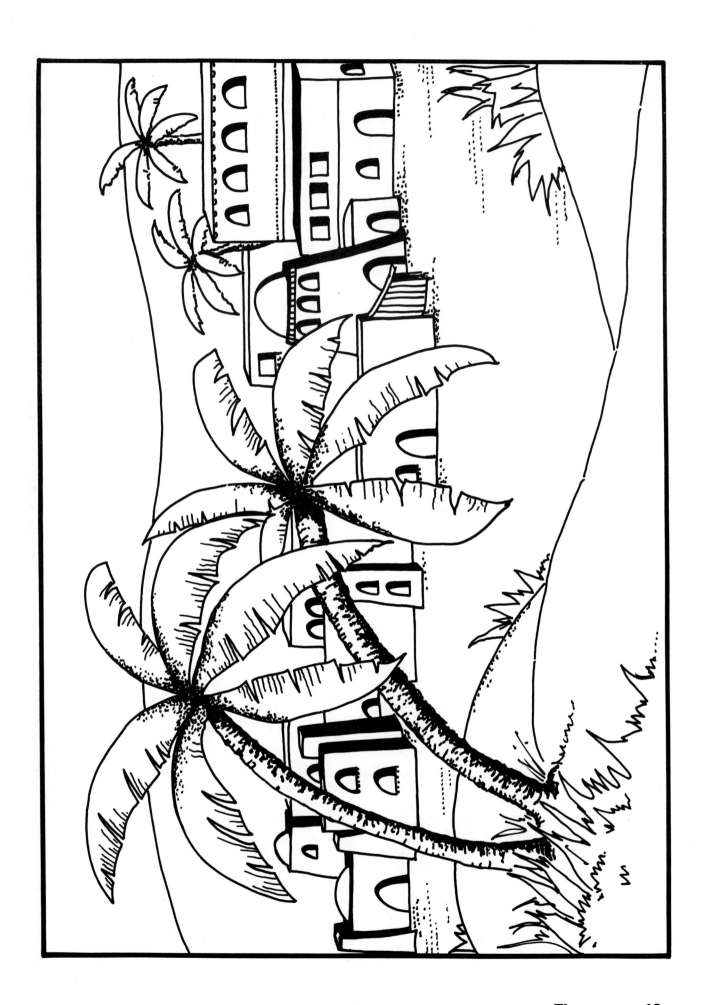

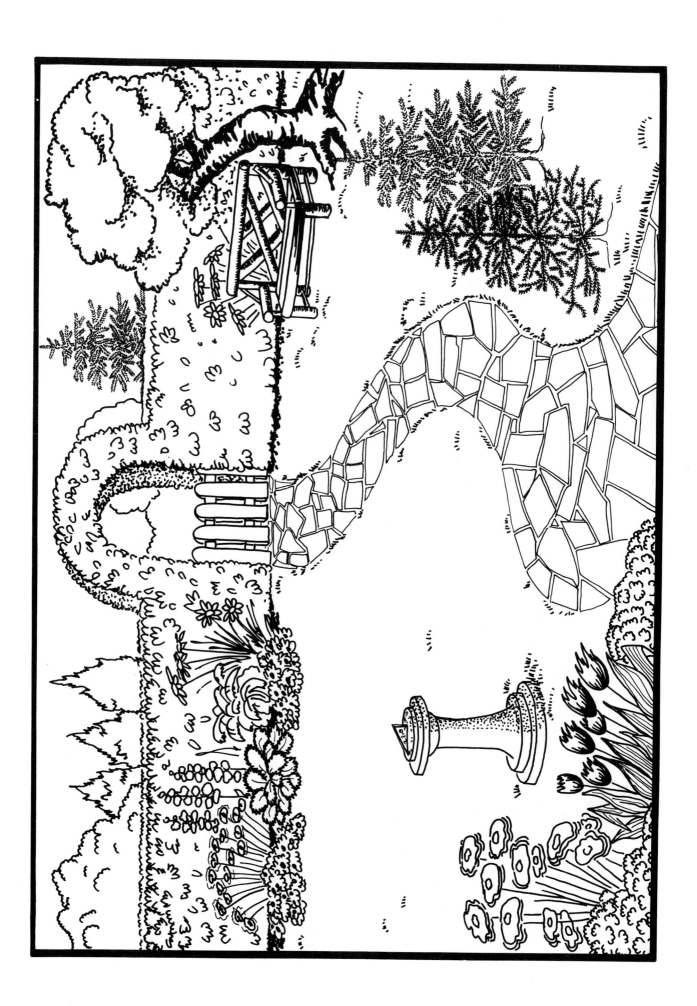

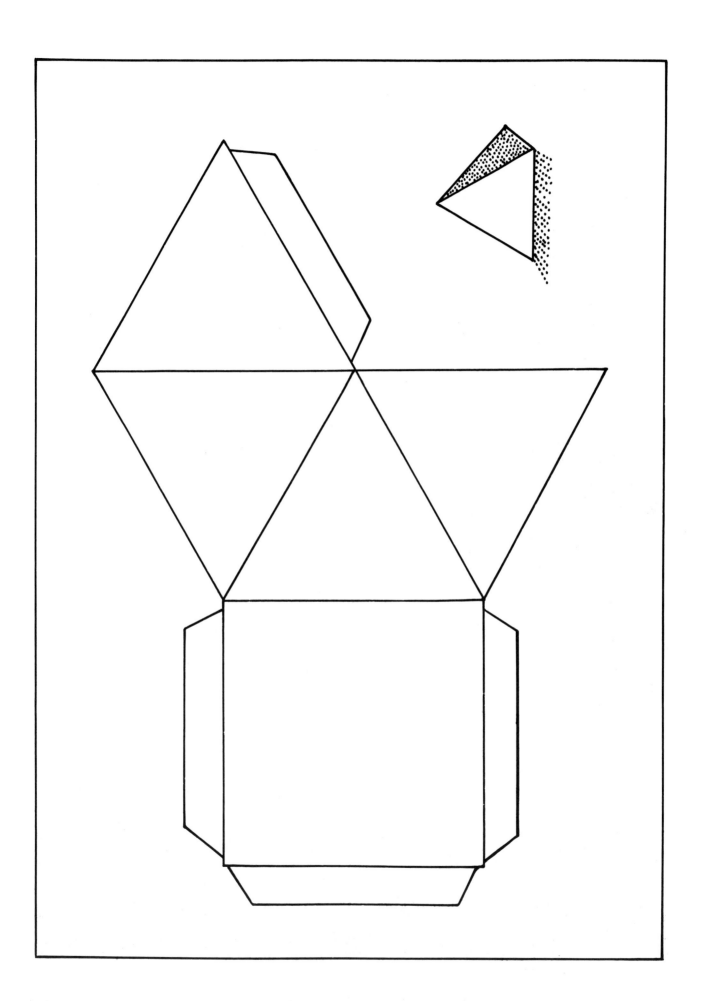

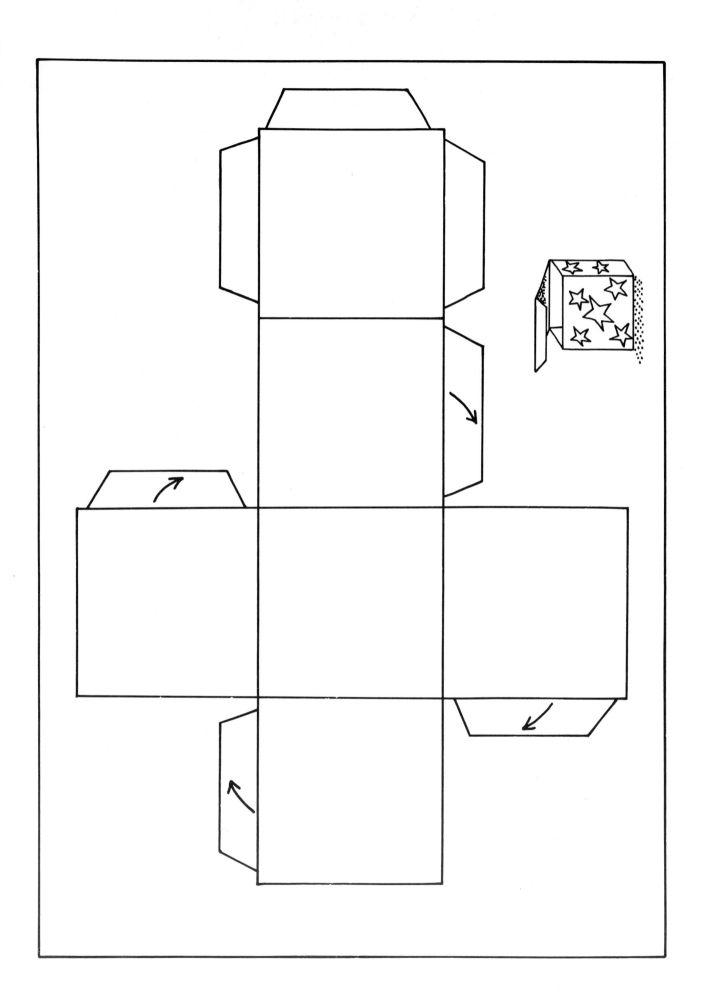

# BLUEPRINTS RESOURCES FOR ART AND FESTIVALS

The **Blueprints** series provides a wide range of carefully structured resources both for art and for the major festivals which compliment *Christmas Art and Craft*. We have reproduced sample pages from some of these books on this and the next page.

*Blueprints: Art Key Stages 1* and *2* provide total coverage of art in the National Curriculum. For each key stage there is a teacher's resource book and a photocopiable book which together provide a complete skill-based, structured resource for developing art in the primary school.

The *Blueprints: Christmas* books for Key Stages 1 and 2 – for infants and juniors respectively – contain a huge bank of materials to make Christmas purposeful and fun and can be used alongside *Christmas Art and Craft*. Each book contains at least three carefully structured Christmas topics, plus photocopiable Christmas plays, songs, poems, games, templates, activity sheets and a wealth of background material.

For other seasons and celebrations there are two more invaluable *Blueprints: Seasonal Topics*, for ideas and activities on the four seasons, and *Blueprints: Festivals*, which covers ten common celebrations: Diwali, Harvest and Thanksgiving, Hallowe'en, Easter, May Day, Chinese New Year, Jewish New Year, Bonfire Night, Ramadan, American Independence Day.

All these books provide a huge bank of highly practical cross-curricular teacher's ideas, which are highly illustrated, plus a large quantity of photocopiable pupil sheets. They are written by practising primary teachers and offer quite unbeatable value for money compared with other comparable resources.

Further information about these and other Stanley Thornes Blueprints books can be obtained from the address and telephone number on the reverse of the title page.

*Reduced pages from* Art Key Stage 2

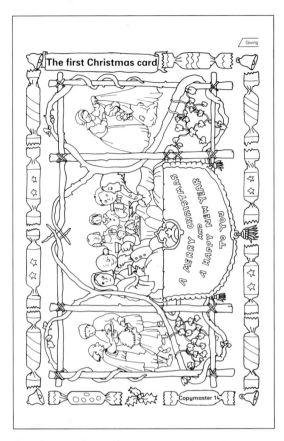

*Reduced pages from* Christmas Key Stage 2

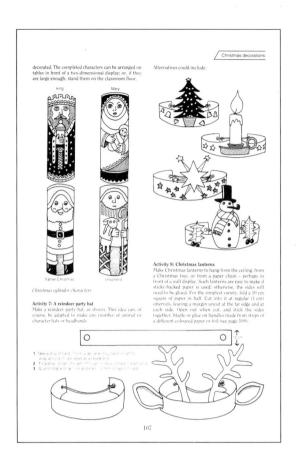

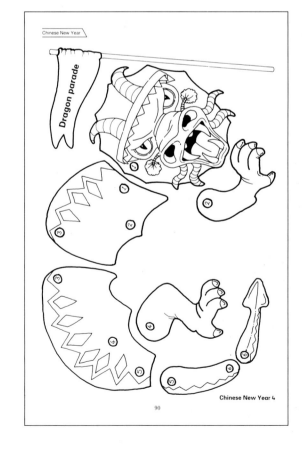

*Reduced Copymasters from* Festivals